www.EffortlessMath.com

... So Much More Online!

✓ FREE Math lessons

✓ More Math learning books!

✓ Mathematics Worksheets

✓ Online Math Tutors

Need a PDF version of this book?

Send email to: Info@EffortlessMath.com

Prepare for the AFOQT Math Test in 7 Days

A Quick Study Guide with Two Full-Length AFOQT Math Practice Tests

By

Reza Nazari & Ava Ross

Copyright © 2019

Reza Nazari & Ava Ross

All rights reserved. No part of this publication may be reproduced, stored in a retrieval system, or transmitted in any form or by any means, electronic, mechanical, photocopying, recording, scanning, or otherwise, except as permitted under Section 107 or 108 of the 1976 United States Copyright Ac, without permission of the author.

All inquiries should be addressed to:

info@effortlessMath.com

www.EffortlessMath.com

ISBN-13: 978-1-64612-134-2

ISBN-10: 1-64612-134-1

Published by: Effortless Math Education

www.EffortlessMath.com

Description

Prepare for the AFOQT Math Test in 7 Days, which reflects the 2019 and 2020 test guidelines and topics, incorporates the best method and the right strategies to help you hone your math skills, overcome your exam anxiety, and boost your confidence -- and do your best to defeat AFOQT Math test quickly. This quick study guide contains only the most important and critical math concepts a student will need in order to succeed on the AFOQT Math test. Math concepts in this book break down the topics, so the material can be quickly grasped. Examples are worked step–by–step to help you learn exactly what to do.

This AFOQT Math new edition has been updated to duplicate questions appearing on the most recent AFOQT Math tests. It contains easy–to–read essential summaries that highlight the key areas of the AFOQT Math test. You only need to spend about 3 – 5 hours daily in your 7–day period in order to achieve your goal. After reviewing this book, you will have solid foundation and adequate practice that is necessary to fully prepare for the AFOQT Math.

Prepare for the AFOQT Math Test in 7 Days is for all AFOQT test takers. It is a breakthrough in Math learning — offering a winning formula and the most powerful methods for learning basic Math topics confidently. Each section offers step–by–step instruction and helpful hints, with a few topics being tackled each day.

Inside the pages of this comprehensive book, students can learn math topics in a structured manner with a complete study program to help them understand essential math skills. It also has many exciting features, including:

- Content 100% aligned with the 2019-2020 AFOQT test
- Written by AFOQT Math tutors and test experts
- Complete coverage of all AFOQT Math concepts and topics which you will be tested
- Step-by-step guide for all AFOQT Math topics
- Dynamic design and easy-to-follow activities
- Over 600 additional AFOQT Math practice questions in both multiple-choice and grid-in formats with answers grouped by topic, so you can focus on your weak areas
- 2 full-length practice tests (featuring new question types) with detailed answers

Effortlessly and confidently follow the step–by–step instructions in this book to prepare for the AFOQT Math in a short period of time.

Prepare for the AFOQT Math Test in 7 Days is the only book you'll ever need to master Basic Math topics! It can be used as a self–study course – you do not need to work with a Math tutor. (It can also be used with a Math tutor).

Ideal for self–study as well as for classroom usage.

About the Author

Reza Nazari is the author of more than 100 Math learning books including:
– **Math and Critical Thinking Challenges:** For the Middle and High School Student
– **GRE Math in 30 Days**
– **AFOQT Math Workbook 2018 - 2019**
– **Effortless Math Education Workbooks**
– and many more Mathematics books …

Reza is also an experienced Math instructor and a test–prep expert who has been tutoring students since 2008. Reza is the founder of Effortless Math Education, a tutoring company that has helped many students raise their standardized test scores—and attend the colleges of their dreams. Reza provides an individualized custom learning plan and the personalized attention that makes a difference in how students view math.

You can contact Reza via email at:
reza@EffortlessMath.com

Find Reza's professional profile at:
goo.gl/zoC9rJ

Contents

Day 1: Fundamental and Building Blocks 9
    Simplifying Fractions 10
    Adding and Subtracting Fractions 10
    Multiplying and Dividing Fractions 11
    Adding Mixed Numbers 11
    Subtracting Mixed Numbers 12
    Multiplying Mixed Numbers 13
    Dividing Mixed Numbers 14
    Rounding Decimals 14
    Adding and Subtracting Decimals 15
    Multiplying and Dividing Decimals 16
    Day 1 Practices 17
    Answers 19

Day 2: Integers, Ratios, and Proportions 20
    Adding and Subtracting Integers 21
    Multiplying and Dividing Integers 21
    Ordering Integers and Numbers 22
    Order of Operations 23
    Integers and Absolute Value 23
    Simplifying Ratios 24
    Proportional Ratios 24
    Create a Proportion 25
    Similarity and Ratios 26
    Day 2 Practices 27
    Answers 29

Day 3: Percentage, Exponents, Variables and Roots 30
    Percentage Calculations 31
    Percent Problems 31
    Percent of Increase and Decrease 32
    Discount, Tax and Tip 32
    Simple Interest 33

Multiplication Property of Exponents...33

Division Property of Exponents..34

Powers of Products and Quotients 35

Zero and Negative Exponents 35

Negative Exponents and Negative Bases 36

Scientific Notation...36

Square Roots 37

Day 3 Practices...38

Answers...40

Day 4: Expressions, Variables, Equations and Inequalities 41

Simplifying Variable Expressions...42

Simplifying Polynomial Expressions 42

The Distributive Property...43

Evaluating One Variable...43

Evaluating Two Variables 44

Combining like Terms...44

One–Step Equations...45

Multi–Step Equations 45

Graphing Single–Variable Inequalities 46

One–Step Inequalities 46

Multi–Step Inequalities 47

Day 4 Practices...48

Answers...50

Day 5: Linear Equations and Inequalities..51

Finding Slope..52

Graphing Lines Using Slope–Intercept Form 52

Graphing Lines Using Standard Form...53

Writing Linear Equations..53

Graphing Linear Inequalities 54

Finding Midpoint...55

Finding Distance of Two Points...55

Day 5 Practices...56

Answers 58

Day 6: Monomials and Polynomials 60

Writing Polynomials in Standard Form 61

Simplifying Polynomials 61

Adding and Subtracting Polynomials 62

Multiplying Monomials 62

Multiplying and Dividing Monomials 63

Multiplying a Polynomial and a Monomial 63

Multiplying Binomials 64

Factoring Trinomials 64

Operations with Polynomials 65

Day 6 Practices 66

Answers 68

Day 7: Geometry and Statistics 69

The Pythagorean Theorem 70

Triangles 70

Polygons 71

Circles 71

Trapezoids 72

Cubes 72

Rectangular Prisms 73

Cylinder 73

Mean, Median, Mode, and Range of the Given Data 74

Pie Graph 74

Probability Problems 75

Day 7 Practices 76

Answers 79

AFOQT Test Review 80

AFOQT Math Practice Tests 81

AFOQT Mathematics Practice Tests Answers and Explanations 108

Day 1: Fundamental and Building Blocks

Math Topics that you'll learn today:

- ✓ Simplifying Fractions
- ✓ Adding and Subtracting Fractions
- ✓ Multiplying and Dividing Fractions
- ✓ Adding Mixed Numbers
- ✓ Subtracting Mixed Numbers
- ✓ Multiplying Mixed Numbers
- ✓ Dividing Mixed Numbers
- ✓ Rounding Decimals
- ✓ Adding and Subtracting Decimals
- ✓ Multiplying and Dividing Decimals

"A Man is like a fraction whose numerator is what he is and whose denominator is what he thinks of himself. The larger the denominator, the smaller the fraction." -Tolstoy

Simplifying Fractions

Step-by-step guide:

✓ Evenly divide both the top and bottom of the fraction by 2, 3, 5, 7, ... etc.

✓ Continue until you can't go any further.

Examples:

1) Simplify $\frac{12}{20}$. To simplify $\frac{12}{20}$, find a number that both 12 and 20 are divisible by. Both are divisible by 4. Then: $\frac{12}{20} = \frac{12 \div 4}{20 \div 4} = \frac{3}{5}$

2) Simplify $\frac{64}{80}$. To simplify $\frac{64}{80}$, find a number that both 64 and 80 are divisible by. Both are divisible by 8 and 16. Then: $\frac{64}{80} = \frac{64 \div 8}{80 \div 8} = \frac{8}{10}$, 8 and 10 are divisible by 2, then: $\frac{8}{10} = \frac{4}{5}$ or $\frac{64}{80} = \frac{64 \div 16}{80 \div 16} = \frac{4}{5}$

Adding and Subtracting Fractions

Step-by-step guide:

✓ For "like" fractions (fractions with the same denominator), add or subtract the numerators and write the answer over the common denominator.

✓ Find equivalent fractions with the same denominator before you can add or subtract fractions with different denominators.

✓ Adding and Subtracting with the same denominator:

$$\frac{a}{b} + \frac{c}{b} = \frac{a+c}{b}, \frac{a}{b} - \frac{c}{b} = \frac{a-c}{b}$$

✓ Adding and Subtracting fractions with different denominators:

$$\frac{a}{b} + \frac{c}{d} = \frac{ad+c}{bd}, \frac{a}{b} - \frac{c}{d} = \frac{ad-cb}{bd}$$

Examples:

1) Calculate. $\frac{4}{5} - \frac{3}{5} =$ $\frac{12}{15} - \frac{9}{15} = \frac{3}{15} = \frac{1}{5}$

   For "like" fractions, subtract the numerators and write the answer over the common denominator. Then: $\frac{4}{5} - \frac{3}{5} = \frac{1}{5}$

2) Subtract fractions. $\frac{2}{3} - \frac{1}{2} =$ $\frac{4}{6} - \frac{3}{6} = 1/6$

   For "unlike" fractions, find equivalent fractions with the same denominator before you can add or subtract fractions with different denominators. Use this formula: $\frac{a}{b} - \frac{c}{d} = \frac{ad - cb}{bd}$

   $\frac{2}{3} - \frac{1}{2} =$

Mult. Fractions — mult. across top divide/simpl.

Divide Fractions — flip 2nd and change to mult.

numerator and denominator of...

Examples:

1) Multiplying fractions. $\frac{5}{6} \times \frac{3}{4} =$ $\frac{15}{24} \div 3 = \frac{5}{8}$

   Multiply the top numbers and multiply the bottom numbers.
   $\frac{5}{6} \times \frac{3}{4} = \frac{5 \times 3}{6 \times 4} = \frac{15}{24}$, simplify: $\frac{15}{24} = \frac{15 \div 3}{24 \div 3} = \frac{5}{8}$

2) Dividing fractions. $\frac{1}{4} \div \frac{2}{3} =$ $\frac{1}{4} \times \frac{3}{2} = \frac{3}{8}$

   Keep first fraction, change division sign to multiplication, and flip the numerator and denominator of the second fraction. Then: $\frac{1}{4} \times \frac{3}{2} = \frac{1 \times 3}{4 \times 2} = \frac{3}{8}$

Adding Mixed Numbers

Prepare for the ASVAB Math Test in 7 Days

Step-by-step guide:

Use the following steps for both adding and subtracting mixed numbers.

- ✓ Add whole numbers of the mixed numbers.
- ✓ Add the fractions of each mixed number.
- ✓ Find the Least Common Denominator (LCD) if necessary.
- ✓ Add whole numbers and fractions.
- ✓ Write your answer in lowest terms.

Examples:

1) Add mixed numbers. $1\frac{3}{4} + 2\frac{3}{8} =$

    [handwritten: $\frac{6}{8} + \frac{3}{8} = \frac{9}{8} = 1\frac{1}{8}$ $\frac{1}{8}$ $3+1=4$]

    Rewriting our equation with parts separated, $1 + \frac{3}{4} + 2 + \frac{3}{8}$, Solving the whole number parts $1 + 2 = 3$, Solving the fraction parts $\frac{3}{4} + \frac{3}{8}$, and rewrite to solve with the equivalent fractions. $\frac{6}{8} + \frac{3}{8} = \frac{9}{8} = 1\frac{1}{8}$, then Combining the whole and fraction parts $3 + 1 + \frac{1}{8} = 4\frac{1}{8}$

2) Add mixed numbers. $1\frac{2}{3} + 4\frac{1}{6} =$

    [handwritten: $1\frac{4}{6} + 4\frac{1}{6} = 5$ $\frac{4}{6} + \frac{1}{6} = 5/6$ $5 5/6$]

    Rewriting our equation with parts separated, $1 + \frac{2}{3} + 4 + \frac{1}{6}$, Solving the whole number parts $1 + 4 = 5$, Solving the fraction parts $\frac{2}{3} + \frac{1}{6}$, and rewrite to solve with the equivalent fractions. $\frac{2}{3} + \frac{1}{6} = \frac{5}{6}$, then Combining the whole and fraction parts $5 + \frac{5}{6} = 5\frac{5}{6}$

Subtracting Mixed Numbers

Step-by-step guide:

Use the following steps for both adding and subtracting mixed numbers.

- ✓ Subtract the whole number of second mixed number from whole number of the first mixed number.
- ✓ Subtract the second fraction from the first one.
- ✓ Find the Least Common Denominator (LCD) if necessary.
- ✓ Add the result of whole numbers and fractions.
- ✓ Write your answer in lowest terms.

Examples:

1) Subtract. $5\frac{2}{3} - 2\frac{1}{4} =$

   Rewriting our equation with parts separated, $5 + \frac{2}{3} - 2 - \frac{1}{4}$

   Solving the whole number parts $5 - 2 = 3$, Solving the fraction parts, $\frac{2}{3} - \frac{1}{4} = \frac{8-3}{12} = \frac{5}{12}$

   Combining the whole and fraction parts, $3 + \frac{5}{12} = 3\frac{5}{12}$

2) Subtract. $3\frac{4}{5} - 1\frac{1}{2} =$

   Rewriting our equation with parts separated, $3 + \frac{4}{5} - 1 - \frac{1}{2}$

   Solving the whole number parts $3 - 1 = 2$, Solving the fraction parts, $\frac{4}{5} - \frac{1}{2} = \frac{3}{10}$

   Combining the whole and fraction parts, $2 + \frac{3}{10} = 2\frac{3}{10}$

Multiplying Mixed Numbers

Step-by-step guide:

✓ Convert the mixed numbers to improper fractions. (improper fraction is a fraction in which the top number is bigger than bottom number)

✓ Multiply fractions and simplify if necessary. $a\frac{c}{b} = a + \frac{c}{b} = \frac{ab+c}{b}$

Examples:

1) Multiply mixed numbers. $3\frac{2}{3} \times 2\frac{1}{2} =$

   Converting mixed numbers to fractions, $3\frac{2}{3} = \frac{11}{3}$ and $2\frac{1}{2} = \frac{5}{2}$.

   $\frac{11}{3} \times \frac{5}{2}$, Applying the fractions formula for multiplication, $\frac{11 \times 5}{3 \times 2} = \frac{55}{6} = 9\frac{1}{6}$

2) Multiply mixed numbers. $4\frac{3}{5} \times 2\frac{1}{3} =$

   Converting mixed numbers to fractions, $\frac{23}{5} \times \frac{7}{3}$, Applying the fractions formula for multiplication, $\frac{23 \times 7}{5 \times 3} = \frac{161}{15} = 10\frac{11}{15}$

Dividing Mixed Numbers

Step-by-step guide:

- ✓ Convert the mixed numbers to improper fractions.
- ✓ Divide fractions and simplify if necessary.

$$a\frac{c}{b} = a + \frac{c}{b} = \frac{ab+c}{b}$$

Examples:

1) Find the quotient. $2\frac{1}{2} \div 1\frac{1}{5} =$

Converting mixed numbers to fractions, $\frac{5}{2} \div \frac{6}{5}$, Applying the fractions formula for multiplication, $\frac{5 \times 5}{2 \times 6} = \frac{25}{12} = 2\frac{1}{12}$

2) Find the quotient. $4\frac{3}{4} \div 3\frac{4}{5} =$

Converting mixed numbers to fractions, $\frac{19}{4} \div \frac{19}{5}$, Applying the fractions formula for multiplication, $\frac{19 \times 5}{4 \times 19} = \frac{95}{76} = 1\frac{1}{4}$

Rounding Decimals

Step-by-step guide:

- ✓ We can round decimals to a certain accuracy or number of decimal places. This is used to make calculation easier to do and results easier to understand, when exact values are not too important.
- ✓ First, you'll need to remember your place values: For example:

$$12.4567$$

| 1: tens | 2: ones | 4: tenths |
| 5: hundredths | 6: thousandths | 7: tens thousandths |

- ✓ To round a decimal, find the place value you'll round to.
- ✓ Find the digit to the right of the place value you're rounding to. If it is 5 or bigger, add 1 to the place value you're rounding to and remove all digits on its right side. If the digit to the right of the place value is less than 5, keep the place value and remove all digits on the right.

Examples:

1) Round 2.183<u>7</u> to the thousandth place value. *2.184*

   First look at the next place value to the right, (tens thousandths). It's 7 and it is greater than 5. Thus add 1 to the digit in the thousandth place.

   Thousandth place is 3. → 3 + 1 = 4, then, the answer is 2.184

2) 2.<u>1837</u> rounded to the nearest hundredth. *2.18*

   First look at the next place value to the right of thousandths. It's 3 and it is less than 5, thus remove all the digits to the right. Then, the answer is 2.18.

Adding and Subtracting Decimals

Step-by-step guide:

- ✓ Line up the numbers.
- ✓ Add zeros to have same number of digits for both numbers if necessary.
- ✓ Add or subtract using column addition or subtraction.

Examples:

1) Add. 2.5 + 1.24 =   *2.5 / 1.24 / 3.74*

   First line up the numbers: $\frac{2.5}{+1.24}$ → Add zeros to have same number of digits for both numbers. $\frac{2.50}{+1.24}$, Start with the hundredths place. 0 + 4 = 4, $\frac{2.50}{+1.24}\over{4}$, Continue with tenths place. 5 + 2 = 7, $\frac{2.50}{+1.24}\over{.74}$. Add the ones place. 2 + 1 = 3, $\frac{2.50}{+1.24}\over{3.74}$

2) Subtract decimals. 4.67 − 2.15 = $\frac{4.67}{-2.15}$ *4.67 / −2.15 / 2.52*

   Start with the hundredths place. 7 − 5 = 2, $\frac{4.67}{-2.15}\over{2}$, continue with tenths place. 6 − 1 = 5 $\frac{4.67}{-2.15}\over{.52}$, subtract the ones place. 4 − 2 = 2, $\frac{4.67}{-2.15}\over{2.52}$.

Multiplying and Dividing Decimals

Step-by-step guide:

For Multiplication:

✓ Ignore the decimal point and set up and multiply the numbers as you do with whole numbers.
Count the total number of decimal places in both of the factors.
Place the decimal point in the product.
For Division:

✓ If the divisor is not a whole number, move decimal point to right to make it a whole number. Do the same for dividend.
✓ Divide similar to whole numbers.

Examples:

1) Find the product. $0.50 \times 0.20 =$

Set up and multiply the numbers as you do with whole numbers. Line up the numbers: $\frac{50}{\times 20}$, Start with the ones place → $50 \times 0 = 0$, $\frac{50}{\times 20} \over 0$, Continue with other digits → $50 \times 2 = 100$, $\frac{50}{\times 20} \over 1,000$, Count the total number of decimal places in both of the factors. (4). Then Place the decimal point in the product.

Then: $\frac{0.50}{\times 0.20} \over 0.1000$ → $0.50 \times 0.20 = 0.1$

2) Find the quotient. $1.20 \div 0.2 =$

The divisor is not a whole number. Multiply it by 10 to get 2. Do the same for the dividend to get 12. Now, divide: $12 \div 2 = 6$. The answer is 6.

mult = right
div = left

Day 1 Practices

✎ *Simplify each fraction.*

1) $\dfrac{27}{54} =$

2) $\dfrac{48}{60} =$

3) $\dfrac{42}{56} =$

4) $\dfrac{30}{120} =$

5) $\dfrac{36}{48} =$

6) $\dfrac{18}{27} =$

✎ *Find the sum or difference.*

7) $\dfrac{12}{19} + \dfrac{7}{19} =$

8) $\dfrac{2}{4} + \dfrac{3}{9} =$

9) $\dfrac{3}{5} + \dfrac{2}{3} =$

10) $\dfrac{3}{7} + \dfrac{2}{3} =$

11) $\dfrac{1}{2} - \dfrac{1}{3} =$

12) $\dfrac{8}{10} - \dfrac{4}{6} =$

✎ *Find the answers.*

13) $\dfrac{3}{6} \times \dfrac{6}{8} =$

14) $\dfrac{1}{5} \times \dfrac{1}{3} =$

15) $\dfrac{1}{4} \times \dfrac{2}{5} =$

16) $\dfrac{1}{6} \times \dfrac{4}{5} =$

17) $\dfrac{1}{5} \times \dfrac{1}{4} =$

18) $\dfrac{2}{5} \times \dfrac{1}{2} =$

✎ *Calculate.*

19) $5\dfrac{1}{2} + 2\dfrac{1}{3} =$

20) $8\dfrac{1}{2} - 3\dfrac{1}{2} =$

21) $5\dfrac{3}{8} + 3\dfrac{1}{8} =$

22) $6\dfrac{1}{2} - 3\dfrac{1}{4} =$

23) $1\dfrac{3}{7} - 1\dfrac{3}{14} =$

24) $7\dfrac{5}{12} + 2\dfrac{3}{4} =$

✏️ **Find the answers.**

25) $4\frac{1}{3} \times 2\frac{1}{5} =$

26) $3\frac{1}{2} \times 3\frac{1}{4} =$

27) $5\frac{2}{5} \div 2\frac{1}{3} =$

28) $2\frac{1}{2} \times 1\frac{2}{9} =$

29) $3\frac{4}{7} \div 2\frac{3}{5} =$

30) $7\frac{2}{3} \div 2\frac{2}{3} =$

✏️ **Round each decimal to the nearest whole number.**

31) 23.48

32) 8.7

33) 14.47

34) 7.5

35) 3.92

36) 56.8

✏️ **Find the sum or difference.**

37) $34.13 - 14.45 =$

38) $37.25 + 22.47 =$

39) $75.50 + 20.78 =$

40) $58.67 - 46.39 =$

41) $73.47 + 14.25 =$

42) $69.99 - 54.61 =$

✏️ **Find the product and quotient.**

43) $0.6 \times 0.3 =$

44) $4.6 \div 0.2 =$

45) $1.25 \times 0.5 =$

46) $0.72 \div 0.2 =$

47) $1.92 \times 0.8 =$

48) $0.52 \div 0.4 =$

Answers

1) $\frac{1}{2}$
2) $\frac{4}{5}$
3) $\frac{3}{4}$
4) $\frac{1}{4}$
5) $\frac{3}{4}$
6) $\frac{2}{3}$
7) $\frac{19}{19} = 1$
8) $\frac{5}{6}$
9) $\frac{19}{15}$
10) $\frac{23}{21}$
11) $\frac{1}{6}$
12) $\frac{2}{15}$
13) $\frac{3}{8}$
14) $\frac{1}{15}$
15) $\frac{1}{10}$
16) $\frac{2}{15}$
17) $\frac{1}{20}$
18) $\frac{1}{5}$
19) $7\frac{5}{6}$
20) 5
21) $8\frac{1}{2}$
22) $3\frac{1}{4}$
23) $\frac{3}{14}$
24) $10\frac{1}{6}$
25) $9\frac{8}{15}$
26) $11\frac{3}{8}$
27) $2\frac{11}{35}$
28) $3\frac{1}{18}$
29) $1\frac{34}{91}$
30) $2\frac{7}{8}$
31) 23
32) 9
33) 14
34) 8
35) 4
36) 57
37) 19.68
38) 59.72
39) 96.28
40) 12.28
41) 87.72
42) 15.38
43) 0.18
44) 23
45) 0.625
46) 3.6
47) 1.536
48) 1.3

Day 2: Integers, Ratios, and Proportions

Math Topics that you'll learn today:

- ✓ Adding and Subtracting Integers
- ✓ Multiplying and Dividing Integers
- ✓ Ordering Integers and Numbers
- ✓ Order of Operations
- ✓ Integers and Absolute Value
- ✓ Simplifying Ratios
- ✓ Proportional Ratios
- ✓ Create a Proportion
- ✓ Similarity and Ratios

"Without mathematics, there's nothing you can do. Everything around you is mathematics. Everything around you is numbers." – Shakuntala Devi

Adding and Subtracting Integers

Step-by-step guide:

- ✓ Integers includes: zero, counting numbers, and the negative of the counting numbers. {... , −3, −2, −1, 0, 1, 2, 3, ...}
- ✓ Add a positive integer by moving to the right on the number line.
- ✓ Add a negative integer by moving to the left on the number line.
- ✓ Subtract an integer by adding its opposite.

Examples:

1) Solve. $(-8) - (-5) =$

   Keep the first number and convert the sign of the second number to its opposite. (change subtraction into addition. Then: $(-8) + 5 = -3$

2) Solve. $10 + (4 - 8) =$

   First subtract the numbers in brackets, $4 - 8 = -4$

   Then: $10 + (-4) = $ → change addition into subtraction: $10 - 4 = 6$

Multiplying and Dividing Integers

Step-by-step guide:

Use these rules for multiplying and dividing integers:

- ✓ (negative) × (negative) = positive
- ✓ (negative) ÷ (negative) = positive
- ✓ (negative) × (positive) = negative
- ✓ (negative) ÷ (positive) = negative
- ✓ (positive) × (positive) = positive

Examples:

1) Solve. $(2 - 5) \times (3) =$

   First subtract the numbers in brackets, $2 - 5 = -3 \rightarrow (-3) \times (3) =$

   Now use this formula: (negative) × (positive) = negative
   $(-3) \times (3) = -9$

2) Solve. $(-12) + (48 \div 6) =$

   First divided 48 by 6, the numbers in brackets, $48 \div 6 = 8$

   $= (-12) + (8) = -12 + 8 = -4$

Ordering Integers and Numbers

Step-by-step guide:

- ✓ When using a number line, numbers increase as you move to the right.
- ✓ When comparing two numbers, think about their position on number line. If one number is on the right side of another number, it is a bigger number. For example, -3 is bigger than -5 because it is on the right side of -5 on number line.

Examples:

1) Order this set of integers from least to greatest. $-2, 1, -5, -1, 2, 4$
   The smallest number is -5 and the largest number is 4.

   Now compare the integers and order them from greatest to least:
   $-5 < -2 < -1 < 1 < 2 < 4$

2) Order each set of integers from greatest to least. $10, -6, -2, 5, -8, 4$
   The largest number is 10 and the smallest number is -8.

   Now compare the integers and order them from least to greatest:
   $10 > 5 > 4 > -2 > -6 > -8$

Order of Operations

Step-by-step guide:

When there is more than one math operation, use PEMDAS:

- ✓ Parentheses
- ✓ Exponents
- ✓ Multiplication and Division (from left to right)
- ✓ Addition and Subtraction (from left to right)

Examples:

1) Solve. $(5 + 7) \div (3^2 \div 3) =$

   First simplify inside parentheses: $(12) \div (9 \div 3) = (12) \div (3) =$
   Then: $(12) \div (3) = 4$

2) Solve. $(11 \times 5) - (12 - 7) =$

   First simplify inside parentheses: $(11 \times 5) - (12 - 7) = (55) - (5) =$

   Then: $(55) - (5) = 50$

Integers and Absolute Value

Step-by-step guide:

- ✓ To find an absolute value of a number, just find its distance from 0 on number line! For example, the distance of 12 and -12 from zero on number line is 12!

Examples:

1) Solve. $\frac{|-18|}{9} \times |5 - 8| =$

   First find $|-18|$, →the absolute value of -18 is 18, then: $|-18| = 18$
   $\frac{18}{9} \times |5 - 8| =$
   Next, solve $|5 - 8|$, → $|5 - 8| = |-3|$, the absolute value of -3 is 3. $|-3| = 3$

Then: $\frac{18}{9} \times 3 = 2 \times 3 = 6$

2) Solve. $|10 - 5| \times \frac{|-2 \times 6|}{3} =$

First solve $|10 - 5|$, $\rightarrow |10 - 5| = |5|$, the absolute value of 5 is 5, $|5| = 5$

$5 \times \frac{|-2 \times 6|}{3} =$

Now solve $|-2 \times 6|$, $\rightarrow |-2 \times 6| = |-12|$, the absolute value of -12 is 12, $|-12| = 12$

Then: $5 \times \frac{12}{3} = 5 \times 4 = 20$

Simplifying Ratios

Step-by-step guide:

- ✓ Ratios are used to make comparisons between two numbers.
- ✓ Ratios can be written as a fraction, using the word "to", or with a colon.
- ✓ You can calculate equivalent ratios by multiplying or dividing both sides of the ratio by the same number.

Examples:

1) Simplify. $8:4 =$

Both numbers 8 and 4 are divisible by 4, $\Rightarrow 8 \div 4 = 2$, $4 \div 4 = 1$,

Then: $8:4 = 2:1$

2) Simplify. $\frac{12}{36} =$

Both numbers 12 and 36 are divisible by 12, $\Rightarrow 12 \div 12 = 1$, $36 \div 12 = 3$,

Then: $\frac{12}{36} = \frac{1}{3}$

Proportional Ratios

Step-by-step guide:

- ✓ A proportion means that two ratios are equal. It can be written in two ways:
$\frac{a}{b} = \frac{c}{d}$, $a:b = c:d$
- ✓ The proportion $\frac{a}{b} = \frac{c}{d}$ can be written as: $a \times d = c \times b$

Examples:

1) Solve this proportion for x. $\frac{4}{8} = \frac{5}{x}$

   Use cross multiplication: $\frac{4}{8} = \frac{5}{x} \Rightarrow 4 \times x = 5 \times 8 \Rightarrow 4x = 40$

   Divide to find x: $x = \frac{40}{4} \Rightarrow x = 10$

2) If a box contains red and blue balls in ratio of $2:3$ red to blue, how many red balls are there if 90 blue balls are in the box?

   Write a proportion and solve. $\frac{2}{3} = \frac{x}{90}$
   Use cross multiplication: $2 \times 90 = 3 \times x \Rightarrow 180 = 3x$
   Divide to find x: $x = \frac{180}{3} \Rightarrow x = 60$

Create a Proportion

Step-by-step guide:

- ✓ A proportion contains two equal fractions! A proportion simply means that two fractions are equal.
- ✓ To create a proportion, simply find (or create) two equal fractions.

Examples:

1) Express ratios as a Proportion.
   120 miles on 4 gallons of gas, how many miles on 1 gallon of gas?

   First create a fraction: $\frac{120 \text{ miles}}{4 \text{ gallons}}$, and divide: $120 \div 4 = 30$

   Then: 30 miles per gallon

2) State if this pair of ratios form a proportion. $\frac{3}{5}$ and $\frac{24}{45}$

   Use cross multiplication: $\frac{3}{5} = \frac{24}{45} \rightarrow 3 \times 45 = 5 \times 24 \rightarrow 135 = 120$, which is not correct.
   Therefore, this pair of ratios doesn't form a proportion.

Similarity and Ratios

Step-by-step guide:

✓ Two or more figures are similar if the corresponding angles are equal, and the corresponding sides are in proportion.

Examples:

1) A girl 160 cm tall, stands 360 cm from a lamp post at night. Her shadow from the light is 90 cm long. How high is the lamp post?

Write the proportion and solve for missing side.
$$\frac{\text{Smaller triangle height}}{\text{Smaller triangle base}} = \frac{\text{Bigger triangle height}}{\text{Bigger triangle base}}$$
$$\Rightarrow \frac{90cm}{160cm} = \frac{90+360cm}{x} \Rightarrow 90x = 160 \times 450 \Rightarrow x = 800 \text{ cm}$$

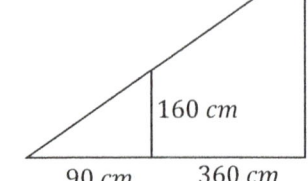

2) A tree 32 feet tall casts a shadow 12 feet long. Jack is 6 feet tall. How long is Jack's shadow?

Write a proportion and solve for the missing number.
$$\frac{32}{12} = \frac{6}{x} \rightarrow 32x = 6 \times 12 = 72$$
$$32x = 72 \rightarrow x = \frac{72}{32} = 2.25 \text{ feet}$$

Day 2 Practices

✎ *Find each sum or difference.*

1) $15 + (-8) =$
2) $(-11) + (-21) =$
3) $7 + (-27) =$
4) $45 + (-14) =$
5) $(-8) + (-12) + 6 =$
6) $37 + (-16) + 12 =$

✎ *Find each product or quotient.*

7) $(-7) \times (-8) =$
8) $4 \times (-5) =$
9) $5 \times (-11) =$
10) $(-5) \times (-20) =$
11) $-(2) \times (-8) \times 3 =$
12) $(12 - 4) \times (-10) =$

✎ *Order each set of integers from least to greatest.*

13) $7, -9, -6, -1, 3$ ___, ___, ___, ___, ___, ___
14) $-4, -11, 5, 12, 9$ ___, ___, ___, ___, ___, ___
15) $18, -12, -19, 21, -20$ ___, ___, ___, ___, ___, ___
16) $-15, -25, 18, -7, 32$ ___, ___, ___, ___, ___, ___

✎ *Evaluate each expression.*

17) $5 + (6 \times 3) =$
18) $13 - (2 \times 5) =$
19) $(14 \times 2) + 18 =$
20) $(12 - 5) - (4 \times 3) =$
21) $25 + (14 \div 2) =$
22) $(18 \times 5) \div 2 =$

✎ **Evaluate the value.**

23) $8 - |4 - 18| - |-2| =$

24) $|-2| - \frac{|-20|}{4} =$

25) $\frac{|-66|}{11} \times |-6| =$

26) $\frac{|-5 \times -3|}{5} \times \frac{|-20|}{4} =$

27) $|2 \times -4| + \frac{|-40|}{5} =$

28) $\frac{|-28|}{4} \times \frac{|-55|}{11} =$

✎ **Reduce each ratio.**

29) $24 : 16 = $ ___ : ___

30) $4 : 40 = $ ___ : ___

31) $6 : 72 = $ ___ : ___

32) $18 : 36 = $ ___ : ___

33) $6 : 100 = $ ___ : ___

34) $4 : 24 = $ ___ : ___

✎ **Solve each proportion.**

35) $\frac{4}{10} = \frac{14}{x}, x = $ ____

36) $\frac{2}{12} = \frac{7}{x}, x = $ ____

37) $\frac{3}{5} = \frac{27}{x}, x = $ ____

38) $\frac{1}{5} = \frac{x}{80}, x = $ ____

39) $\frac{3}{7} = \frac{x}{63}, x = $ ____

40) $\frac{2}{8} = \frac{13}{x}, x = $ ____

✎ **State if each pair of ratios form a proportion.**

41) $\frac{6}{20}$ and $\frac{9}{30}$

42) $\frac{1}{2}$ and $\frac{16}{32}$

43) $\frac{10}{12}$ and $\frac{35}{42}$

44) $\frac{3}{7}$ and $\frac{27}{72}$

45) $\frac{2}{5}$ and $\frac{16}{45}$

46) $\frac{8}{18}$ and $\frac{40}{81}$

✎ **Solve each problem.**

47) Two rectangles are similar. The first is 6 *feet* wide and 20 *feet* long. The second is 15 *feet* wide. What is the length of the second rectangle? _____

48) Two rectangles are similar. One is 2.5 *meters* by 9 *meters*. The longer side of the second rectangle is 22.5 *meters*. What is the other side of the second rectangle? _____

Answers

1) 7
2) −32
3) −20
4) 31
5) −14
6) 33
7) 56
8) −20
9) −55
10) 100
11) 48
12) −80
13) −9, −6, −1, 3, 7
14) −11, −4, 5, 9, 12
15) −20, −19, −12, 18, 21
16) −25, −15, −7, 18, 32

17) 23
18) 3
19) 46
20) −5
21) 32
22) 45
23) −8
24) −3
25) 36
26) 15
27) 16
28) 35
29) 3 : 2
30) 1 : 10
31) 1 : 12
32) 1 : 2

33) 3 : 50
34) 1 : 6
35) 35
36) 42
37) 45
38) 16
39) 27
40) 52
41) Yes
42) Yes
43) Yes
44) No
45) No
46) No
47) 50 feet
48) 6.25 meters

Day 3:
Percentage, Exponents, Variables and Roots

Math Topics that you'll learn today:

- ✓ Percentage Calculations
- ✓ Percent Problems
- ✓ Percent of Increase and Decrease
- ✓ Discount, Tax and Tip
- ✓ Simple Interest
- ✓ Multiplication Property of Exponents
- ✓ Division Property of Exponents
- ✓ Powers of Products and Quotients
- ✓ Zero and Negative Exponents
- ✓ Negative Exponents and Negative Bases
- ✓ Scientific Notation
- ✓ Square Roots

Mathematics is no more computation than typing is literature. - John Allen Paulos

Percentage Calculations

Step-by-step guide:

- ✓ Percent is a ratio of a number and 100. It always has the same denominator, 100. Percent symbol is %.
- ✓ Percent is another way to write decimals or fractions. For example:
$$40\% = 0.40 = \frac{40}{100} = \frac{2}{5}$$
- ✓ Use the following formula to find part, whole, or percent:
$$\text{part} = \frac{\text{percent}}{100} \times \text{whole}$$

Examples:

1) What is 10% of 45? Use the following formula: $\text{part} = \frac{\text{percent}}{100} \times \text{whole}$

$\text{part} = \frac{10}{100} \times 45 \rightarrow \text{part} = \frac{1}{10} \times 45 \rightarrow \text{part} = \frac{45}{10} \rightarrow \text{part} = 4.5$

2) What is 15% of 24? Use the percent formula: $\text{part} = \frac{\text{percent}}{100} \times \text{whole}$

$\text{part} = \frac{15}{100} \times 24 \rightarrow \text{part} = \frac{360}{100} \rightarrow \text{part} = 3.6$

Percent Problems

Step-by-step guide:

- ✓ In each percent problem, we are looking for the base, or part or the percent.
- ✓ Use the following equations to find each missing section.
    - ○ Base = Part ÷ Percent
    - ○ Part = Percent × Base
    - ○ Percent = Part ÷ Base

Examples:

1) 1.2 is what percent of 24?
   In this problem, we are looking for the percent. Use the following equation:
   $Percent = Part \div Base \rightarrow Percent = 1.2 \div 24 = 0.05 = 5\%$

2) 20 is 5% of what number?

Use the following formula: $Base = Part \div Percent \rightarrow Base = 20 \div 0.05 = 400$
20 is 5% of 400.

Percent of Increase and Decrease

Step-by-step guide:

To find the percentage of increase or decrease:
- ✓ New Number – Original Number
- ✓ The result ÷ Original Number × 100
- ✓ If your answer is a negative number, then this is a percentage decrease. If it is positive, then this is a percent of increase.

Examples:

1) Increased by 50%, the numbers 84 becomes:

    First find 50% of 84 → $\frac{50}{100} \times 84 = \frac{50 \times 84}{100} = 42$

    Then: $84 + 42 = 126$

2) The price of a shirt increases from \$10 to \$14. What is the percent increase?
    First: $14 - 10 = 4$
    4 is the result. Then: $4 \div 10 = \frac{4}{10} = 0.4 = 40\%$

Discount, Tax and Tip

Step-by-step guide:

- ✓ Discount = Multiply the regular price by the rate of discount
- ✓ Selling price = original price – discount
- ✓ Tax: To find tax, multiply the tax rate to the taxable amount (income, property value, etc.)
- ✓ To find tip, multiply the rate to the selling price.

Examples:

1) With an 10% discount, Ella was able to save \$20 on a dress. What was the original price of the dress?
    $10\% \: of \: x = 20, \frac{10}{100} \times x = 20, x = \frac{100 \times 20}{10} = 200$

2) Sophia purchased a sofa for $530.40. The sofa is regularly priced at $624. What was the percent discount Sophia received on the sofa?
Use this formula: $percent = Part \div base = 530.40 \div 624 = 0.85 = 85\%$
Therefore, the discount is: $100\% - 85\% = 15\%$

Simple Interest

Step-by-step guide:

- ✓ Simple Interest: The charge for borrowing money or the return for lending it. To solve a simple interest problem, use this formula:
Interest = principal x rate x time ⇒ $I = p \times r \times t$

Examples:

1) Find simple interest for $450 investment at 7% for 8 years.
Use Interest formula: $I = prt$, $P = \$450$, $r = 7\% = \frac{7}{100} = 0.07$ and $t = 8$
Then: $I = 450 \times 0.07 \times 8 = \$252$

2) Find simple interest for $5,200 at 4% for 3 years.
Use Interest formula: $I = prt$, $P = \$5,200$, $r = 4\% = \frac{4}{100} = 0.04$ and $t = 3$
Then: $I = 5,200 \times 0.04 \times 3 = \$624$

Multiplication Property of Exponents

Step-by-step guide:

- ✓ Exponents are shorthand for repeated multiplication of the same number by itself. For example, instead of 2×2, we can write 2^2. For $3 \times 3 \times 3 \times 3$, we can write 3^4
- ✓ In algebra, a variable is a letter used to stand for a number. The most common letters are: $x, y, z, a, b, c, m,$ and n.
- ✓ Exponent's rules: $x^a \times x^b = x^{a+b}$, $\frac{x^a}{x^b} = x^{a-b}$

$$(x^a)^b = x^{a \times b}, \qquad (xy)^a = x^a \times y^a, \left(\frac{a}{b}\right)^c = \frac{a^c}{b^c}$$

Examples:

1) Multiply. $-2x^5 \times 7x^3 =$
   Use Exponent's rules: $x^a \times x^b = x^{a+b} \rightarrow x^5 \times x^3 = x^{5+3} = x^8$
   Then: $-2x^5 \times 7x^3 = -14x^8$

2) Multiply. $(x^2y^4)^3 =$
   Use Exponent's rules: $(x^a)^b = x^{a \times b}$. Then: $(x^2y^4)^3 = x^{2 \times 3}y^{4 \times 3} = x^6y^{12}$

Division Property of Exponents

Step-by-step guide:

✓ For division of exponents use these formulas: $\frac{x^a}{x^b} = x^{a-b}$, $x \neq 0$

$$\frac{x^a}{x^b} = \frac{1}{x^{b-a}}, x \neq 0, \qquad \frac{1}{x^b} = x^{-b}$$

Examples:

1) Simplify. $\frac{4x^3y}{36x^2y^3} =$

   First cancel the common factor: $4 \rightarrow \frac{4x^3y}{36x^2y^3} = \frac{x^3y}{9x^2y^3}$

   Use Exponent's rules: $\frac{x^a}{x^b} = x^{a-b} \rightarrow \frac{x^3}{x^2} = x^{3-2}$

   Then: $\frac{4x^3y}{36x^2y^3} = \frac{xy}{9y^3} \rightarrow$ now cancel the common factor: $y \rightarrow \frac{xy}{9y^3} = \frac{x}{9y^2}$

2) Divide. $\frac{2x^{-5}}{9x^{-2}} =$

   Use Exponent's rules: $\frac{x^a}{x^b} = \frac{1}{x^{b-a}} \rightarrow \frac{x^{-5}}{x^{-2}} = \frac{1}{x^{-2-(-5)}} = \frac{1}{x^{-2+5}} = \frac{1}{x^3}$

   Then: $\frac{2x^{-5}}{9x^{-2}} = \frac{2}{9x^3}$

Powers of Products and Quotients

Step-by-step guide:

- ✓ For any nonzero numbers a and b and any integer x, $(ab)^x = a^x \times b^x$.

Examples:

1) Simplify. $(3x^5y^4)^2 =$

   Use Exponent's rules: $(x^a)^b = x^{a \times b}$

   $(3x^5y^4)^2 = (3)^2(x^5)^2(y^4)^2 = 9x^{5 \times 2}y^{4 \times 2} = 9x^{10}y^8$

2) Simplify. $(\frac{2x}{3x^2})^2 =$ First cancel the common factor: $x \rightarrow (\frac{2x}{3x^2})^2 = (\frac{2}{3x})^2$

   Use Exponent's rules: $(\frac{a}{b})^c = \frac{a^c}{b^c}$, Then: $(\frac{2}{3x})^2 = \frac{2^2}{(3x)^2} = \frac{4}{9x^2}$

Zero and Negative Exponents

Step-by-step guide:

- ✓ A negative exponent simply means that the base is on the wrong side of the fraction line, so you need to flip the base to the other side. For instance, "x^{-2}" (pronounced as "ecks to the minus two") just means "x^2" but underneath, as in $\frac{1}{x^2}$.

Examples:

1) Evaluate. $(\frac{4}{9})^{-2} =$

   Use Exponent's rules: $\frac{1}{x^b} = x^{-b} \rightarrow (\frac{4}{9})^{-2} = \frac{1}{(\frac{4}{9})^2} = \frac{1}{\frac{4^2}{9^2}}$

   Now use fraction rule: $\frac{1}{\frac{b}{c}} = \frac{c}{b} \rightarrow \frac{1}{\frac{4^2}{9^2}} = \frac{9^2}{4^2} = \frac{81}{16}$

2) Evaluate. $(\frac{5}{6})^{-3} =$

   Use Exponent's rules: $\frac{1}{x^b} = x^{-b} \rightarrow (\frac{5}{6})^{-3} = \frac{1}{(\frac{5}{6})^3} = \frac{1}{\frac{5^3}{6^3}}$, Now use fraction rule: $\frac{1}{\frac{b}{c}} = \frac{c}{b} \rightarrow \frac{1}{\frac{5^3}{6^3}} = \frac{6^3}{5^3} = \frac{216}{125}$

Negative Exponents and Negative Bases

Step-by-step guide:

- ✓ Make the power positive. A negative exponent is the reciprocal of that number with a positive exponent.
- ✓ The parenthesis is important!
- ✓ 5^{-2} is not the same as $(-5)^{-2}$

$$(-5)^{-2} = -\frac{1}{5^2} \text{ and } (-5)^{-2} = +\frac{1}{5^2}$$

Examples:

1) Simplify. $\left(\frac{3a}{2c}\right)^{-2} =$

   Use Exponent's rules: $\frac{1}{x^b} = x^{-b} \rightarrow \left(\frac{3a}{2c}\right)^{-2} = \frac{1}{\left(\frac{3a}{2c}\right)^2} = \frac{1}{\frac{3^2 a^2}{2^2 c^2}}$

   Now use fraction rule: $\frac{1}{\frac{b}{c}} = \frac{c}{b} \rightarrow \frac{1}{\frac{3^2 a^2}{2^2 c^2}} = \frac{2^2 c^2}{3^2 a^2}$

   Then: $\frac{2^2 c^2}{3^2 a^2} = \frac{4c^2}{9a^2}$

2) Simplify. $\left(-\frac{5x}{3yz}\right)^{-3} =$

   Use Exponent's rules: $\frac{1}{x^b} = x^{-b} \rightarrow \left(-\frac{5x}{3yz}\right)^{-3} = \frac{1}{\left(-\frac{5x}{3yz}\right)^3} = \frac{1}{-\frac{5^3 x^3}{3^3 y^3 z^3}}$

   Now use fraction rule: $\frac{1}{\frac{b}{c}} = \frac{c}{b} \rightarrow \frac{1}{-\frac{5^3 x^3}{3^3 y^3 z^3}} = -\frac{3^3 y^3 z^3}{5^3 x^3} = -\frac{27 y^3 z^3}{125 x^3}$

Scientific Notation

Step-by-step guide:

- ✓ It is used to write very big or very small numbers in decimal form.
- ✓ In scientific notation all numbers are written in the form of:

$$m \times 10^n$$

Decimal notation	Scientific notation
5	5×10^0
$-25,000$	-2.5×10^4
0.5	5×10^{-1}
2,122.456	$2,122456 \times 10^3$

Examples:

1) Write 0.00012 in scientific notation.

   First, move the decimal point to the right so that you have a number that is between 1 and 10. Then: $N = 1.2$

   Second, determine how many places the decimal moved in step 1 by the power of 10. Then: 10^{-4} → When the decimal moved to the right, the exponent is negative.

   Then: $0.00012 = 1.2 \times 10^{-4}$

2) Write 8.3×10^{-5} in standard notation.

   10^{-5} → When the decimal moved to the right, the exponent is negative.

   Then: $8.3 \times 10^{-5} = 0.000083$

Square Roots

Step-by-step guide:

- ✓ A square root of x is a number r whose square is: $r^2 = x$

   r is a square root of x.

Examples:

1) Find the square root of $\sqrt{225}$.

   First factor the number: $225 = 15^2$, Then: $\sqrt{225} = \sqrt{15^2}$

   Now use radical rule: $\sqrt[n]{a^n} = a$

   Then: $\sqrt{15^2} = 15$

2) Evaluate. $\sqrt{4} \times \sqrt{16} =$

   First factor the numbers: $4 = 2^2$ and $16 = 4^2$

   Then: $\sqrt{4} \times \sqrt{16} = \sqrt{2^2} \times \sqrt{4^2}$

   Now use radical rule: $\sqrt[n]{a^n} = a$, Then: $\sqrt{2^2} \times \sqrt{4^2} = 2 \times 4 = 8$

Day 3 Practices

✍ *Calculate the given percent of each value.*

1) 5% of 60 = ____
2) 10% of 30 = ____
3) 20% of 25 = ____
4) 50% of 80 = ____
5) 40% of 200 = ____
6) 20% of 45 = ____

✍ *Solve each problem.*

7) 20 is what percent of 50? ____%
8) 18 is what percent of 90? ____%
9) 12 is what percent of 15? ____%
10) 16 is what percent of 200? ____%
11) 24 is what percent of 800? ____%
12) 48 is what percent of 400? ____%

✍ *Solve each percent of change word problem.*

13) Bob got a raise, and his hourly wage increased from $12 to $15. What is the percent increase? _____ %

14) The price of a pair of shoes increases from $20 to $32. What is the percent increase? ____ %

✍ *Find the selling price of each item.*

15) Original price of a computer: $500
Tax: 6%, Selling price: $_____

16) Original price of a laptop: $350
Tax: 8%, Selling price: $_____

✍ *Determine the simple interest for these loans.*

17) $1,300 at 5% for 6 years. $ _____

18) $5,400 at 3.5% for 6 months. $ _____

✍ *Simplify and write the answer in exponential form.*

19) $2yx^3 \times 4x^2y^3 =$
20) $4x^2 \times 9x^3y^4 =$
21) $7x^4y^5 \times 3x^2y^3 =$
22) $9x^2y^5 \times 7xy^3 =$
23) $4xy^4 \times 7x^3y^3 =$
24) $8x^2y^3 \times 3x^5y^3 =$

✏️ Simplify. (Division Property of Exponents)

25) $\frac{3^7 \times 3^4}{3^8 \times 3^2} =$

26) $\frac{5x}{10x^3} =$

27) $\frac{6x^3}{4x^5} =$

28) $\frac{24x^3}{28x^6} =$

29) $\frac{24x^3}{18y^8} =$

30) $\frac{50xy^4}{10y^2} =$

✏️ Simplify. (Powers of Products and Quotients)

31) $(9x^7y^5)^2 =$

32) $(4x^4y^6)^5 =$

33) $(3x \times 4y^3)^2 =$

34) $(\frac{5x}{x^2})^2 =$

35) $\left(\frac{x^4y^4}{x^2y^2}\right)^3 =$

36) $\left(\frac{25x}{5x^6}\right)^2 =$

✏️ Evaluate the following expressions. (Zero and Negative Exponents)

37) $2^{-3} =$

38) $3^{-3} =$

39) $7^{-3} =$

40) $6^{-3} =$

41) $8^{-3} =$

42) $9^{-2} =$

✏️ Simplify. (Negative Exponents and Negative Bases)

43) $-5x^{-2}y^{-3} =$

44) $20x^{-4}y^{-1} =$

45) $14a^{-6}b^{-7} =$

46) $-12x^2y^{-3} =$

47) $-\frac{25}{x^{-6}} =$

48) $\frac{7b}{-9c^{-4}} =$

✏️ Write each number in scientific notation.

49) $0.000325 =$

50) $0.00023 =$

51) $56,000,000 =$

52) $21,000 =$

✏️ Evaluate.

53) $\sqrt{9} \times \sqrt{4} =$ _____

54) $\sqrt{64} \times \sqrt{25} =$ _____

55) $\sqrt{8} \times \sqrt{2} =$ _____

56) $\sqrt{6} \times \sqrt{6} =$ _____

57) $\sqrt{5} \times \sqrt{5} =$ _____

58) $\sqrt{8} \times \sqrt{8} =$ _____

Answers

1) 3
2) 3
3) 5
4) 40
5) 80
6) 9
7) 40%
8) 20%
9) 80%
10) 8%
11) 3%
12) 12%
13) 25%
14) 60%
15) $530.00
16) $378.00
17) $390.00
18) $94.50
19) $8x^5y^4$
20) $36x^5y^4$
21) $21x^6y^8$
22) $63x^3y^8$
23) $28x^4y^7$
24) $24x^7y^6$
25) 3
26) $\frac{1}{2x^2}$
27) $\frac{3}{2x^2}$
28) $\frac{6}{7x^3}$
29) $\frac{4x^3}{3y^8}$
30) $5xy^2$
31) $81x^{14}y^{10}$
32) $1{,}024x^{20}y^{30}$
33) $144x^2y^6$
34) $\frac{25}{x^2}$
35) x^6y^6
36) $\frac{25}{x^{10}}$
37) $\frac{1}{8}$
38) $\frac{1}{27}$
39) $\frac{1}{343}$
40) $\frac{1}{216}$
41) $\frac{1}{512}$
42) $\frac{1}{81}$
43) $-\frac{5}{x^2y^3}$
44) $\frac{20}{x^4y}$
45) $\frac{14}{a^6b^7}$
46) $-\frac{12x^2}{y^3}$
47) $-25x^6$
48) $-\frac{7bc^4}{9}$
49) 3.25×10^{-4}
50) 2.3×10^{-4}
51) 5.6×10^7
52) 2.1×10^4
53) 6
54) 40
55) 4
56) 6
57) 5
58) 8

Day 4: Expressions, Variables, Equations and Inequalities

Math Topics that you'll learn today:

- ✓ Simplifying Variable Expressions
- ✓ Simplifying Polynomial Expressions
- ✓ The Distributive Property
- ✓ Evaluating One Variable
- ✓ Evaluating Two Variables
- ✓ Combining like Terms
- ✓ One–Step Equations
- ✓ Multi–Step Equations
- ✓ Graphing Single–Variable Inequalities
- ✓ One–Step Inequalities
- ✓ Multi–Step Inequalities

Mathematics is, as it were, a sensuous logic, and relates to philosophy as do the arts, music, and plastic art to poetry. – K. Shegel

Simplifying Variable Expressions

Step-by-step guide:

- In algebra, a variable is a letter used to stand for a number. The most common letters are: $x, y, z, a, b, c, m,$ and n.
- algebraic expression is an expression contains integers, variables, and the math operations such as addition, subtraction, multiplication, division, etc.
- In an expression, we can combine "like" terms. (values with same variable and same power)

Examples:

1) Simplify this expression. $(10x + 2x + 3) =?$
   Combine like terms. Then: $(10x + 2x + 3) = 12x + 3$ (remember you cannot combine variables and numbers.
2) Simplify this expression. $12 - 3x^2 + 9x + 5x^2 =?$
   Combine "like" terms: $-3x^2 + 5x^2 = 2x^2$
   Then: $12 - 3x^2 + 9x + 5x^2 = 12 + 2x^2 + 9x$. Write in standard form (biggest powers first): $2x^2 + 9x + 12$

Simplifying Polynomial Expressions

Step-by-step guide:

- In mathematics, a polynomial is an expression consisting of variables and coefficients that involves only the operations of addition, subtraction, multiplication, and non-negative integer exponents of variables.
$$P(x) = a_n x^n + a_{n-1} x^{n-1} + \ldots + a_2 x^2 + a_1 x + a_0$$

Examples:

1) Simplify this Polynomial Expressions. $4x^2 - 5x^3 + 15x^4 - 12x^3 =$
   Combine "like" terms: $-5x^3 - 12x^3 = -17x^3$
   Then: $4x^2 - 5x^3 + 15x^4 - 12x^3 = 4x^2 - 17x^3 + 15x^4$
   Then write in standard form: $4x^2 - 17x^3 + 15x^4 = 15x^4 - 17x^3 + 4x^2$

2) Simplify this expression. $(2x^2 - x^4) - (4x^4 - x^2) =$
   First use distributive property: → multiply $(-)$ into $(4x^4 - x^2)$
   $(2x^2 - x^4) - (4x^4 - x^2) = 2x^2 - x^4 - 4x^4 + x^2$

Then combine "like" terms: $2x^2 - x^4 - 4x^4 + x^2 = 3x^2 - 5x^4$

And write in standard form: $3x^2 - 5x^4 = -5x^4 + 3x^2$

The Distributive Property

Step-by-step guide:

✓ Distributive Property: $a(b + c) = ab + ac$

Examples:

1) Simply. $(5x - 3)(-5) =$

   Use Distributive Property formula: $a(b + c) = ab + ac$
   $(5x - 3)(-5) = -25x + 15$

2) Simply $(-8)(2x - 8) =$

   Use Distributive Property formula: $a(b + c) = ab + ac$
   $(-8)(2x - 8) = -16x + 64$

Evaluating One Variable

Step-by-step guide:

✓ To evaluate one variable expression, find the variable and substitute a number for that variable.
✓ Perform the arithmetic operations.

Examples:

1) Solve this expression. $12 - 2x, x = -1$

   First substitute -1 for x, then:

   $12 - 2x = 12 - 2(-1) = 12 + 2 = 14$

2) Solve this expression. $-8 + 5x, x = 3$

   First substitute 3 for x, then: $-8 + 5x = -8 + 5(3) = -8 + 15 = 7$

Evaluating Two Variables

Step-by-step guide:

- ✓ To evaluate an algebraic expression, substitute a number for each variable and perform the arithmetic operations.

Examples:

1) Solve this expression. $-3x + 5y$, $x = 2$, $y = -1$

   First substitute 2 for x, and -1 for y, then:
   $-3x + 5y = -3(2) + 5(-1) = -6 - 5 = -11$

2) Solve this expression. $2(a - 2b)$, $a = -1$, $b = 3$

   First substitute -1 for a, and 3 for b, then:
   $2(a - 2b) = 2a - 4b = 2(-1) - 4(3) = -2 - 12 = -14$

Combining like Terms

Step-by-step guide:

- ✓ Terms are separated by "+" and "-" signs.
- ✓ Like terms are terms with same variables and same powers.
- ✓ Be sure to use the "+" or "-" that is in front of the coefficient.

Examples:

1) Simplify this expression. $(-5)(8x - 6) =$

   Use Distributive Property formula: $a(b + c) = ab + ac$
   $(-5)(8x - 6) = -40x + 30$

2) Simplify this expression. $(-3)(2x - 2) + 6 =$

   First use Distributive Property formula: $a(b + c) = ab + ac$
   $(-3)(2x - 2) + 6 = -6x + 6 + 6$

   And Combining like Terms:

   $-6x + 6 + 6 = -6x + 12$

One–Step Equations

Step-by-step guide:

- ✓ The values of two expressions on both sides of an equation are equal. $ax + b = c$
- ✓ You only need to perform one Math operation in order to solve the one-step equations.
- ✓ To solve one-step equation, find the inverse (opposite) operation is being performed.
- ✓ The inverse operations are:
    - Addition and subtraction
    - Multiplication and division

Examples:

1) Solve this equation. $x + 24 = 0, x = ?$
   Here, the operation is addition and its inverse operation is subtraction. To solve this equation, subtract 24 from both sides of the equation: $x + 24 - 24 = 0 - 24$
   Then simplify: $x + 24 - 24 = 0 - 24 \rightarrow x = -24$

2) Solve this equation. $3x = 15, x = ?$
   Here, the operation is multiplication (variable x is multiplied by 3) and its inverse operation is division. To solve this equation, divide both sides of equation by 3:
   $$3x = 15 \rightarrow 3x \div 3 = 15 \div 3 \rightarrow x = 5$$

Multi–Step Equations

Step-by-step guide:

- ✓ Combine "like" terms on one side.
- ✓ Bring variables to one side by adding or subtracting.
- ✓ Simplify using the inverse of addition or subtraction.
- ✓ Simplify further by using the inverse of multiplication or division.

Examples:

1) Solve this equation. $-(2 - x) = 5$
   First use Distributive Property: $-(2 - x) = -2 + x$
   Now solve by adding 2 to both sides of the equation. $-2 + x = 5 \rightarrow -2 + x + 2 = 5 + 2$

Now simplify: $-2 + x + 2 = 5 + 2 \rightarrow x = 7$

2) Solve this equation. $4x + 10 = 25 - x$

First bring variables to one side by adding x to both sides.
$4x + 10 + x = 25 - x + x \rightarrow 5x + 10 = 25$. Now, subtract 10 from both sides:
$5x + 10 - 10 = 25 - 10 \rightarrow 5x = 15$
Now, divide both sides by 5: $5x = 15 \rightarrow 5x \div 5 = \frac{15}{5} \rightarrow x = 3$

Graphing Single–Variable Inequalities

Step-by-step guide:

- ✓ Inequality is similar to equations and uses symbols for "less than" (<) and "greater than" (>).
- ✓ To solve inequalities, we need to isolate the variable. (like in equations)
- ✓ To graph an inequality, find the value of the inequality on the number line.
- ✓ For less than or greater than draw open circle on the value of the variable.
- ✓ If there is an equal sign too, then use filled circle.
- ✓ Draw a line to the right or to the left for greater or less than.

Examples:

1) Draw a graph for $x > 2$

Since, the variable is greater than 2, then we need to find 2 and draw an open circle above it. Then, draw a line to the right.

2) Graph this inequality. $x < 5$

One–Step Inequalities

Step-by-step guide:

- ✓ Similar to equations, first isolate the variable by using inverse operation.
- ✓ For dividing or multiplying both sides by negative numbers, flip the direction of the inequality sign.

Examples:

1) Solve and graph the inequality. $x + 2 \geq 3$.

Subtract 2 from both sides. $x + 2 \geq 3 \rightarrow x + 2 - 2 \geq 3 - 2$, then: $x \geq 1$

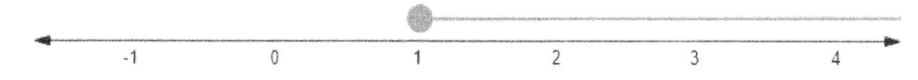

2) Solve this inequality. $x - 1 \leq 2$

Add 1 to both sides. $x - 1 \leq 2 \rightarrow x - 1 + 1 \leq 2 + 1$, then: $x \leq 3$

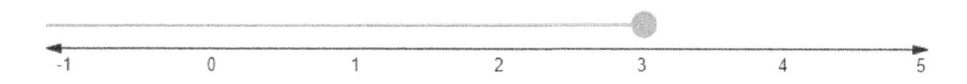

Multi–Step Inequalities

Step-by-step guide:

- ✓ Isolate the variable.
- ✓ Simplify using the inverse of addition or subtraction.
- ✓ Simplify further by using the inverse of multiplication or division.

Examples:

1) Solve this inequality. $2x - 2 \leq 6$

   First add 2 to both sides: $2x - 2 + 2 \leq 6 + 2 \rightarrow 2x \leq 8$

   Now, divide both sides by 2: $2x \leq 8 \rightarrow x \leq 4$

2) Solve this inequality. $2x - 4 \leq 8$

   First add 4 to both sides: $2x - 4 + 4 \leq 8 + 4$

   Then simplify: $2x - 4 + 4 \leq 8 + 4 \rightarrow 2x \leq 12$

   Now divide both sides by 2: $\frac{2x}{2} \leq \frac{12}{2} \rightarrow x \leq 6$

Day 4 Practices

✏️ *Simplify each expression.*

1) $(2x + x + 8 + 19) =$

2) $(-22x - 26x + 24) =$

3) $8x + 3 - 4x =$

4) $-2 - 5x^2 - 2x^2 =$

5) $3 + 10x^2 + 2 =$

6) $3x^2 + 6x + 12x^2 =$

✏️ *Simplify each polynomial.*

7) $(2x^3 + 5x^2) - (12x + 2x^2) =$ _____

8) $(2x^5 + 2x^3) - (7x^3 + 6x^2) =$ _____

9) $(12x^4 + 4x^2) - (2x^2 - 6x^4) =$ _____

✏️ *Use the distributive property to simply each expression.*

10) $2(2 + 3x) =$

11) $3(5 + 5x) =$

12) $4(3x - 8) =$

13) $(6x - 2)(-2) =$

14) $(-3)(x + 2) =$

15) $(2 + 2x)5 =$

✏️ *Evaluate each expression using the value given.*

16) $5 + x, x = 2$

17) $x - 2, x = 4$

18) $8x + 1, x = 9$

19) $x - 12, x = -1$

20) $9 - x, x = 3$

21) $x + 2, x = 5$

✏️ *Evaluate each expression using the values given.*

22) $2x + 4y, x = 3, y = 2$

23) $8x + 5y, x = 1, y = 5$

24) $-2a + 4b, a = 6, b = 3$

25) $4x + 7 - 2y, x = 7, y = 6$

✍ *Simplify each expression. (Combining like Terms)*

26) $2x + x + 2 =$

27) $2(5x - 3) =$

28) $7x - 2x + 8 =$

29) $(-4)(3x - 5) =$

30) $9x - 7x - 5 =$

31) $16x - 5 + 8x =$

✍ *Solve each equation. (One–Step Equations)*

32) $16 = -4 + x, x =$ ____

33) $x - 4 = -25, x =$ ____

34) $x + 12 = -9, x =$ ____

35) $14 = 18 - x, x =$ ____

36) $2 + x = -14, x =$ ____

37) $x - 5 = 15, x =$ ____

✍ *Solve each equation. (Multi–Step Equations)*

38) $-3(2 + x) = 3$

39) $-2(4 + x) = 4$

40) $20 = -(x - 8)$

41) $2(2 - 2x) = 20$

42) $-12 = -(2x + 8)$

43) $5(2 + x) = 5$

✍ *Draw a graph for each inequality.*

44) $x > -1$

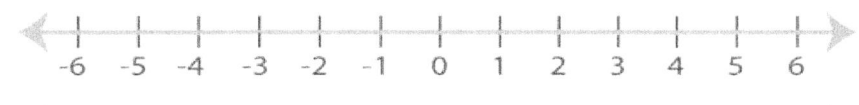

45) $x < 3$

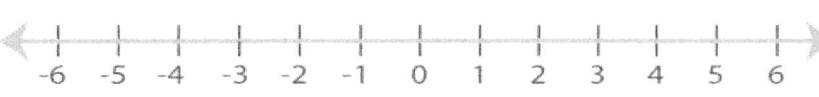

✍ *Solve each inequality and graph it.*

46) $2x \geq 12$

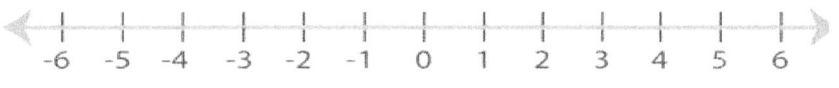

47) $4 + x \leq 5$

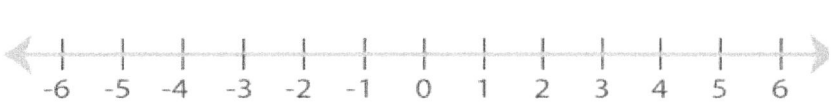

✍ *Solve each inequality.*

48) $4x - 16 \leq 12$

49) $16x - 4 \leq 28$

50) $-15 + 9x \leq 30$

51) $2(x - 3) \leq 6$

52) $14x - 10 \leq 18$

53) $8x - 42 < 38$

Answers

1) $3x + 27$
2) $-48x + 24$
3) $4x + 3$
4) $-7x^2 - 2$
5) $10x^2 + 5$
6) $15x^2 + 6x$
7) $2x^3 + 3x^2 - 12x$
8) $2x^5 - 5x^3 - 6x^2$
9) $18x^4 + 2x^2$
10) $6x + 4$
11) $15x + 15$
12) $12x - 32$
13) $-12x + 4$
14) $-3x - 6$
15) $10x + 10$
16) 7
17) 2
18) 73
19) -13
20) 6
21) 7
22) 14
23) 33
24) 0
25) 23
26) $3x + 2$
27) $10x - 6$
28) $5x + 8$
29) $-12x + 20$
30) $2x - 5$
31) $24x - 5$
32) 20
33) -21
34) -21
35) 4
36) -16
37) 20
38) -3
39) -6
40) -12
41) -4
42) 2
43) -1

44) [number line: open circle at -1, shaded to the right]

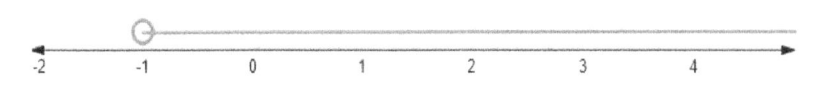

45) [number line: open circle at 3, shaded to the left]

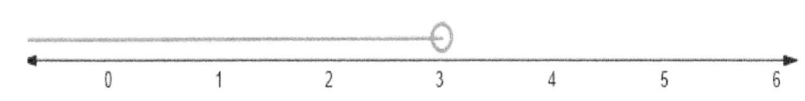

46) [number line: closed circle at 6, shaded to the right]

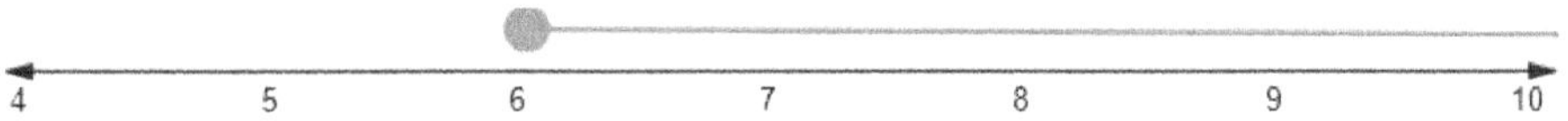

47) [number line: closed circle at 1, shaded to the left]

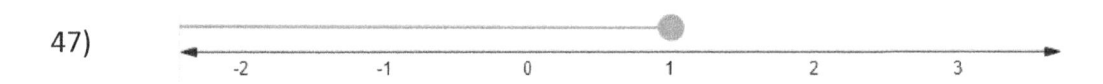

48) $x \leq 7$
49) $x \leq 2$
50) $x \leq 5$
51) $x \leq 6$
52) $x \leq 2$
53) $x < 10$

Day 5:
Linear Equations and Inequalities

Math Topics that you'll learn today:

- ✓ Finding Slope
- ✓ Graphing Lines Using Slope–Intercept Form
- ✓ Graphing Lines Using Standard Form
- ✓ Writing Linear Equations
- ✓ Graphing Linear Inequalities
- ✓ Finding Midpoint
- ✓ Finding Distance of Two Points

"Nature is written in mathematical language." - Galileo Galilei

Finding Slope

Step-by-step guide:

- ✓ The slope of a line represents the direction of a line on the coordinate plane.
- ✓ A coordinate plane contains two perpendicular number lines. The horizontal line is x and the vertical line is y. The point at which the two axes intersect is called the origin. An ordered pair (x, y) shows the location of a point.
- ✓ A line on coordinate plane can be drawn by connecting two points.
- ✓ To find the slope of a line, we need two points.
- ✓ The slope of a line with two points A (x_1, y_1) and B (x_2, y_2) can be found by using this formula: $\frac{y_2 - y_1}{x_2 - x_1} = \frac{rise}{run}$

Examples:

1) Find the slope of the line through these two points: $(2, -10)$ and $(3, 6)$.

   Slope $= \frac{y_2 - y_1}{x_2 - x_1}$. Let (x_1, y_1) be $(2, -10)$ and (x_2, y_2) be $(3, 6)$. Then: slope $= \frac{y_2 - y_1}{x_2 - x_1} = \frac{6 - (-10)}{3 - 2} = \frac{6 + 10}{1} = \frac{16}{1} = 16$

2) Find the slope of the line containing two points $(8, 3)$ and $(-4, 9)$.

   Slope $= \frac{y_2 - y_1}{x_2 - x_1} \rightarrow (x_1, y_1) = (8, 3)$ and $(x_2, y_2) = (-4, 9)$. Then: slope $= \frac{y_2 - y_1}{x_2 - x_1} = \frac{9 - 3}{-4 - 8} = \frac{6}{-12} = \frac{1}{-2} = -\frac{1}{2}$

Graphing Lines Using Slope–Intercept Form

Step-by-step guide:

- ✓ Slope-intercept form of a line: given the slope m and the y-intercept (the intersection of the line and y-axis) b, then the equation of the line is:
$$y = mx + b$$

Example: Sketch the graph of $y = 8x - 3$.

To graph this line, we need to find two points. When x is zero the value of y is -3. And when y is zero the value of x is 3/8. $x = 0 \rightarrow y = 8(0) - 3 = -3$, $y = 0 \rightarrow 0 = 8x - 3 \rightarrow x = \frac{3}{8}$

Now, we have two points: $(0,-3)$ and $(\frac{3}{8},0)$. Find the points and graph the line. Remember that the slope of the line is 8.

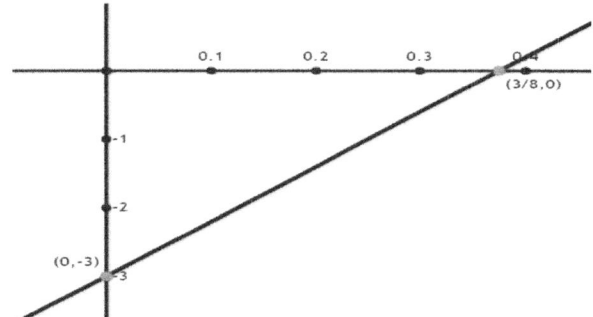

Graphing Lines Using Standard Form

Step-by-step guide:

- ✓ Find the x–intercept of the line by putting zero for y.
- ✓ Find the y–intercept of the line by putting zero for the x.
- ✓ Connect these two points.

Examples:

Sketch the graph of $x - y = -5$.

First isolate y for x: $x - y = -5 \rightarrow y = x + 5$
Find the x-intercept of the line by putting zero for y.
$y = x + 5 \rightarrow x + 5 = 0 \rightarrow x = -5$

Find the y-intercept of the line by putting zero for the x.
$y = 0 + 5 \rightarrow y = 5$

Then: x-intercept: $(-5,0)$ and y-intercept: $(0,5)$

Writing Linear Equations

Step-by-step guide:

- ✓ The equation of a line: $y = mx + b$
- ✓ Identify the slope.
- ✓ Find the y-intercept. This can be done by substituting the slope and the

coordinates of a point (x, y) on the line.

Examples:

1) What is the equation of the line that passes through $(2, -2)$ and has a slope of 7?
   The general slope-intercept form of the equation of a line is $y = mx + b$, where m is the slope and b is the y-intercept.
   By substitution of the given point and given slope, we have: $-2 = (2)(7) + b$
   So, $b = -2 - 14 = -16$, and the required equation is $y = 7x - 16$.

2) Write the equation of the line through $(2, 1)$ and $(-1, 4)$.
   $Slop = \frac{y_2 - y_1}{x_2 - x_1} = \frac{4-1}{-1-2} = \frac{3}{-3} = -1 \rightarrow m = -1$
   To find the value of b, you can use either points. The answer will be the same: $y = -x + b$
   $(2, 1) \rightarrow 1 = -2 + b \rightarrow b = 3$
   $(-1, 4) \rightarrow 4 = -(-1) + b \rightarrow b = 3$
   The equation of the line is: $y = -x + 3$

Graphing Linear Inequalities

Step-by-step guide:

- ✓ First, graph the "equals" line.
- ✓ Choose a testing point. (it can be any point on both sides of the line.)
- ✓ Put the value of (x, y) of that point in the inequality. If that works, that part of the line is the solution. If the values don't work, then the other part of the line is the solution.

Examples:

Sketch the graph of $y < 2x - 3$. First, graph the line:

$y = 2x - 3$. The slope is 2 and y-intercept is -3. Then, choose a testing point. The easiest point to test is the origin: $(0, 0)$

$$(0,0) \rightarrow y < 2x - 3 \rightarrow 0 < 2(0) - 3 \rightarrow 0 < -3$$

0 is not less than -3. So, the other part of the line (on the right side) is the solution.

Finding Midpoint

Step-by-step guide:

- ✓ The middle of a line segment is its midpoint.
- ✓ The Midpoint of two endpoints A (x_1, y_1) and B (x_2, y_2) can be found using this formula: $M(\frac{x_1+x_2}{2}, \frac{y_1+y_2}{2})$

Example:

1) Find the midpoint of the line segment with the given endpoints. $(4, -5), (0, 9)$

   Midpoint = $(\frac{x_1+x_2}{2}, \frac{y_1+y_2}{2}) \rightarrow (x_1, y_1) = (4, -5)$ and $(x_2, y_2) = (0, 9)$

   Midpoint = $(\frac{4+0}{2}, \frac{-5+9}{2}) \rightarrow (\frac{4}{2}, \frac{4}{2}) \rightarrow M(2, 2)$

2) Find the midpoint of the line segment with the given endpoints. $(6, 7), (4, -5)$

   Midpoint = $(\frac{x_1+x_2}{2}, \frac{y_1+y_2}{2}) \rightarrow (x_1, y_1) = (6, 7)$ and $(x_2, y_2) = (4, -5)$

   Midpoint = $(\frac{6+4}{2}, \frac{7-5}{2}) \rightarrow (\frac{10}{2}, \frac{2}{2}) \rightarrow (5, 1)$

Finding Distance of Two Points

Step-by-step guide:

- ✓ Distance of two points A (x_1, y_1) and B (x_2, y_2): $d = \sqrt{(x_1 - x_2)^2 + (y_1 - y_2)^2}$

Examples:

1) Find the distance between of $(0, 8), (-4, 5)$.

   Use distance of two points formula: $d = \sqrt{(x_1 - x_2)^2 + (y_1 - y_2)^2}$
   $(x_1, y_1) = (0, 8)$ and $(x_2, y_2) = (-4, 5)$. Then: $d = \sqrt{(x_1 - x_2)^2 + (y_1 - y_2)^2} \rightarrow$
   $d = \sqrt{(0 - (-4))^2 + (8 - 5)^2} = \sqrt{(4)^2 + (3)^2} = \sqrt{16 + 9} = \sqrt{25} = 5 \rightarrow d = 5$

2) Find the distance of two points $(4, 2)$ and $(-5, -10)$.

   Use distance of two points formula: $d = \sqrt{(x_1 - x_2)^2 + (y_1 - y_2)^2}$
   $(x_1, y_1) = (4, 2)$, and $(x_2, y_2) = (-5, -10)$
   Then: $d = \sqrt{(x_1 - x_2)^2 + (y_1 - y_2)^2} \rightarrow d = \sqrt{(4 - (-5))^2 + (2 - (-10))^2} =$
   $\sqrt{(9)^2 + (12)^2} = \sqrt{81 + 144} = \sqrt{225} = 15$. Then: $d = 15$

Day 5 Practices

✎ *Find the slope of the line through each pair of points.*

1) $(1, 4), (3, 8)$
2) $(-1, 5), (0, 6)$
3) $(5, -5), (4, -1)$
4) $(-2, -1), (0, 5)$
5) $(5, 1), (2, 4)$
6) $(-3, 5), (-2, 8)$

✎ *Sketch the graph of each line. (Using Slope–Intercept Form)*

7) $y = \frac{1}{2}x - 4$

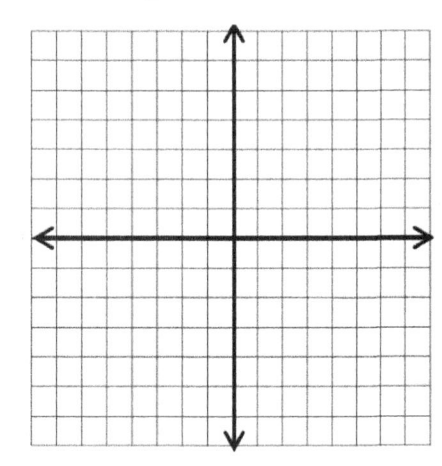

8) $y = 2x$

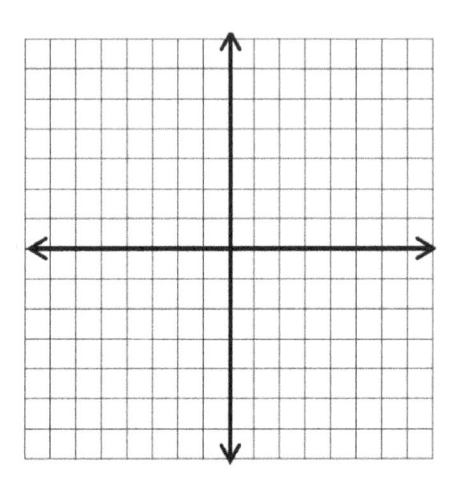

✎ *Sketch the graph of each line. (Graphing Lines Using Standard Form)*

9) $y = 3x - 2$

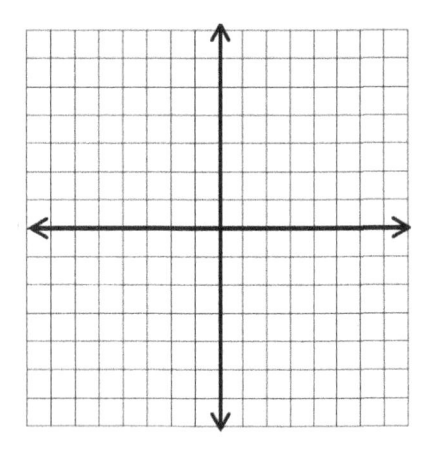

10) $y = -x + 1$

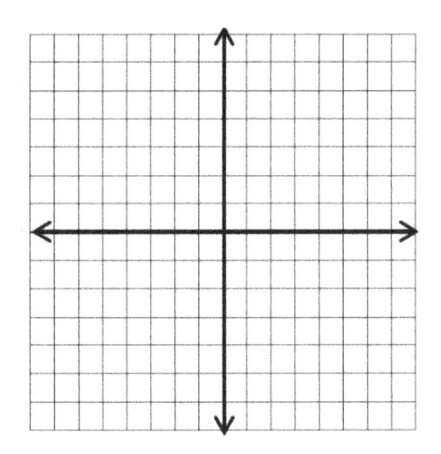

✏ *Write the equation of the line through the given points.*

11) through: $(1, -2), (-2, -17)$
12) through: $(-2, 1), (3, 6)$
13) through: $(-2, 1), (0, 5)$
14) through: $(5, 4), (2, 1)$
15) through: $(-4, 9), (3, 2)$
16) through: $(1, 0), (5, 20)$

✏ *Sketch the graph of each linear inequality. (Graphing Linear Inequalities)*

17) $2y > 6x - 2$

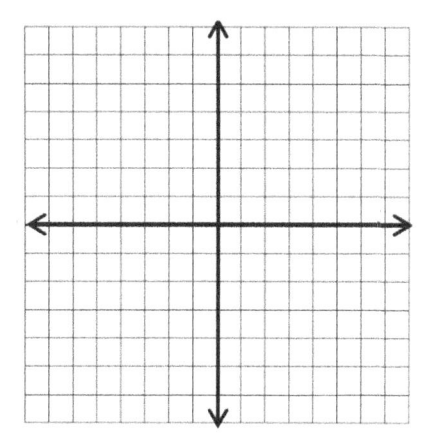

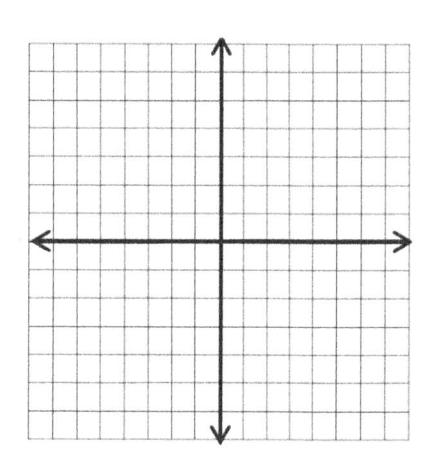

18) $3y < -3x + 12$

✏ *Find the midpoint of the line segment with the given endpoints.*

19) $(-4, -6), (2, 6)$
20) $(7, 4), (-4, 1)$
21) $(-4, -1), (8, 3)$
22) $(-5, 2), (1, 6)$
23) $(3, -2), (7, -6)$
24) $(-7, -3), (5, -7)$

✏ *Find the distance between each pair of points.*

25) $(5, -1), (2, -5)$
26) $(-4, -1), (0, 2)$
27) $(-4, 2), (2, 10)$
28) $(-1, -6), (4, 6)$
29) $(3, -2), (-6, -14)$
30) $(-3, 0), (1, 3)$

Answers

Find the slope of the line through each pair of points.

1) 2
2) 1
3) −4
4) 3
5) −1
6) 3

Sketch the graph of each line. (Using Slope–Intercept Form)

7)

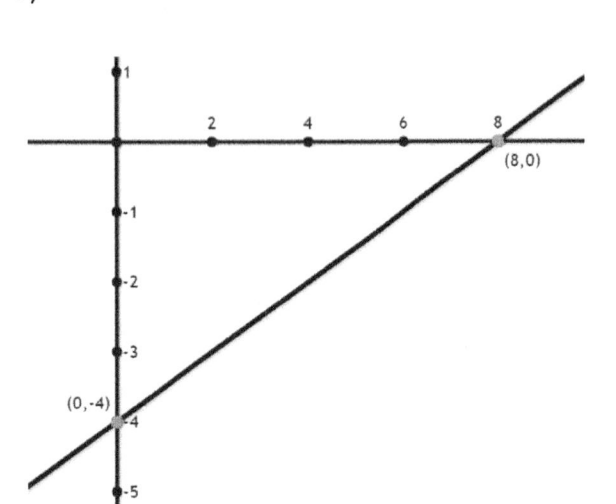

8)

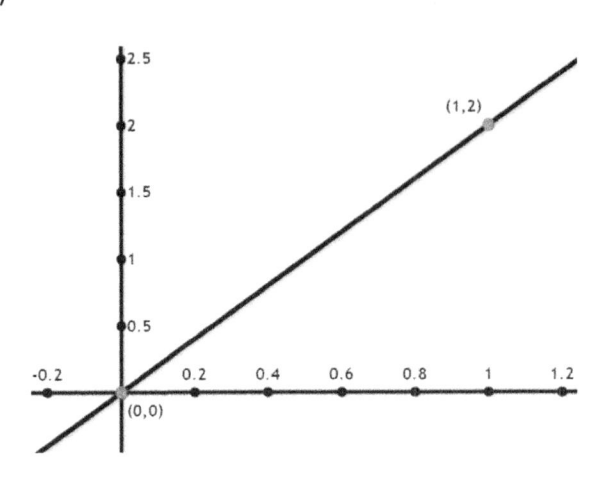

Sketch the graph of each line. (Graphing Lines Using Standard Form)

9) $y = 3x - 2$

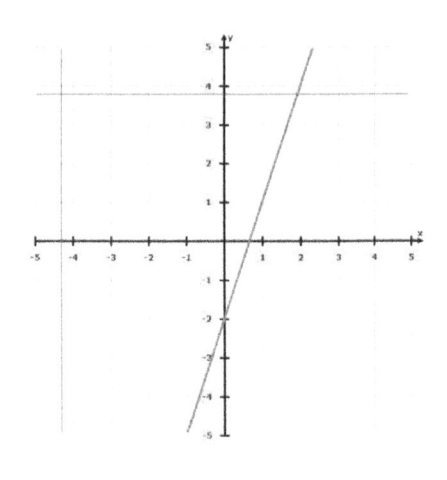

10) $y = -x + 1$

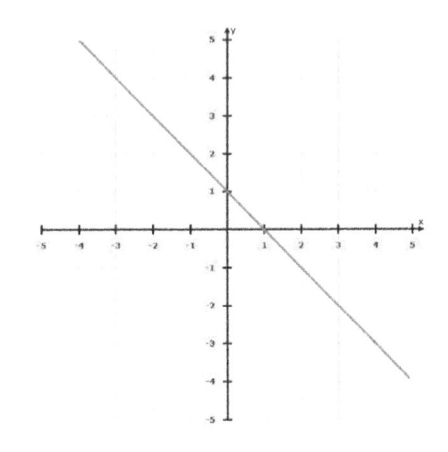

Write the equation of the line through the given points.

11) $y = 5x - 7$
12) $y = x + 3$
13) $y = 2x + 5$

14) $y = x - 1$
15) $y = -x + 5$
16) $y = 5x - 5$

Sketch the graph of each linear inequality. (Graphing Linear Inequalities)

17) $y > 3x - 1$

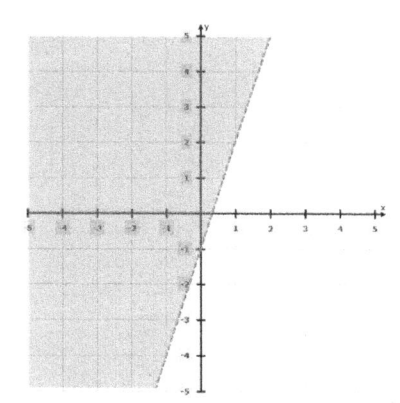

18) $y < -x + 4$

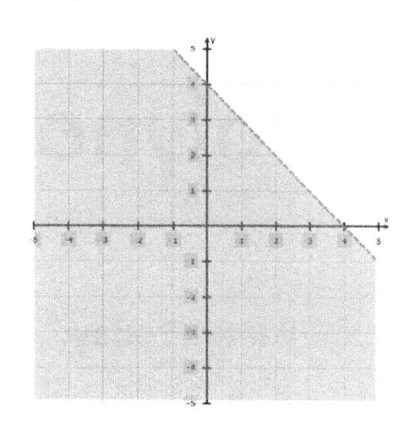

Find the midpoint of the line segment with the given endpoints.

19) $(-1, 0)$
20) $(1.5, 2.5)$
21) $(2, 1)$

22) $(-2, 4)$
23) $(5, -4)$
24) $(-1, -5)$

Find the distance between each pair of points.

25) 5
26) 5
27) 10

28) 13
29) 15
30) 5

Day 6: Monomials and Polynomials

Math Topics that you'll learn today:

- ✓ Writing Polynomials in Standard Form
- ✓ Simplifying Polynomials
- ✓ Adding and Subtracting Polynomials
- ✓ Multiplying Monomials
- ✓ Multiplying and Dividing Monomials
- ✓ Multiplying a Polynomial and a Monomial
- ✓ Multiplying Binomials
- ✓ Factoring Trinomials
- ✓ Operations with Polynomials

Mathematics is the supreme judge: from its decisions there is no appeal. –Tobias Dantzig

Writing Polynomials in Standard Form

Step-by-step guide:

- ✓ A polynomial function $f(x)$ of degree n is of the form
$$f(x) = a_n x^n + a_{n-1} x_{n-1} + \cdots + a_1 x + a_0$$
- ✓ The first term is the one with the biggest power!

Examples:

1) Write this polynomial in standard form. $-12 + 3x^2 - 6x^4 =$

    The first term is the one with the biggest power: $-12 + 3x^2 - 6x^4 = -6x^4 + 3x^2 - 12$

2) Write this polynomial in standard form. $5x^2 - 9x^5 + 8x^3 - 11 =$

    The first term is the one with the biggest power: $5x^2 - 9x^5 + 8x^3 - 11 =$
    $-9x^5 + 8x^3 + 5x^2 - 11$

Simplifying Polynomials

Step-by-step guide:

- ✓ Find "like" terms. (they have same variables with same power).
- ✓ Use "FOIL". (First-Out-In-Last) for binomials:
$$(x + a)(x + b) = x^2 + (b + a)x + ab$$
- ✓ Add or Subtract "like" terms using order of operation.

Examples:

1) Simplify this expression. $4x(6x - 3) =$

    Use Distributive Property: $4x(6x - 3) = 24x^2 - 12x$

2) Simplify this expression. $(6x - 2)(2x - 3) =$

    First apply FOIL method: $(a + b)(c + d) = ac + ad + bc + bd$
    $(6x - 2)(2x - 3) = 12x^2 - 18x - 4x + 6$
    Now combine like terms: $12x^2 - 18x - 4x + 6 = 12x^2 - 22x + 6$

Adding and Subtracting Polynomials

Step-by-step guide:

- ✓ Adding polynomials is just a matter of combining like terms, with some order of operations considerations thrown in.
- ✓ Be careful with the minus signs, and don't confuse addition and multiplication!

Examples:

1) Simplify the expressions. $(4x^3 + 3x^4) - (x^4 - 5x^3) =$

   First use Distributive Property for $-(x^4 - 5x^3)$, → $-(x^4 - 5x^3) = -x^4 + 5x^3$

   $(4x^3 + 3x^4) - (x^4 - 5x^3) = 4x^3 + 3x^4 - x^4 + 5x^3$

   Now combine like terms: $4x^3 + 3x^4 - x^4 + 5x^3 = 2x^4 + 9x^3$

2) Add expressions. $(2x^3 - 6) + (9x^3 - 4x^2) =$

   Remove parentheses: $(2x^3 - 6) + (9x^3 - 4x^2) = 2x^3 - 6 + 9x^3 - 4x^2$

   Now combine like terms: $2x^3 - 6 + 9x^3 - 4x^2 = 11x^3 - 4x^2 - 6$

Multiplying Monomials

Step-by-step guide:

- ✓ A monomial is a polynomial with just one term, like $2x$ or $7y$.

Examples:

1) Multiply expressions. $5a^4b^3 \times 2a^3b^2 =$

   Use this formula: $x^a \times x^b = x^{a+b}$

   $a^4 \times a^3 = a^{4+3} = a^7$ and $b^3 \times b^2 = b^{3+2} = b^5$, Then: $5a^4b^3 \times 2a^3b^2 = 10a^7b^5$

2) Multiply expressions. $-4xy^4z^2 \times 3x^2y^5z^3 =$

   Use this formula: $x^a \times x^b = x^{a+b}$ → $x \times x^2 = x^{1+2} = x^3$, $y^4 \times y^5 = y^{4+5} = y^9$

   and $z^2 \times z^3 = z^{2+3} = z^5$, Then: $-4xy^4z^2 \times 3x^2y^5z^3 = -12x^3y^9z^5$

Multiplying and Dividing Monomials

Step-by-step guide:

- ✓ When you divide two monomials you need to divide their coefficients and then divide their variables.
- ✓ In case of exponents with the same base, you need to subtract their powers.
- ✓ Exponent's rules:

$$x^a \times x^b = x^{a+b}, \quad \frac{x^a}{x^b} = x^{a-b}$$
$$\frac{1}{x^b} = x^{-b}, \quad (x^a)^b = x^{a \times b}$$
$$(xy)^a = x^a \times y^a$$

Examples:

1) Multiply expressions. $(-3x^7)(4x^3) =$
   Use this formula: $x^a \times x^b = x^{a+b} \rightarrow x^7 \times x^3 = x^{10}$
   Then: $(-3x^7)(4x^3) = -12x^{10}$

2) Dividing expressions. $\frac{18x^2y^5}{2xy^4} =$
   Use this formula: $\frac{x^a}{x^b} = x^{a-b}$, $\frac{x^2}{x} = x^{2-1} = x$ and $\frac{y^5}{y^4} = y^{5-4} = y$
   Then: $\frac{18x^2y^5}{2xy^4} = 9xy$

Multiplying a Polynomial and a Monomial

Step-by-step guide:

- ✓ When multiplying monomials, use the product rule for exponents.
- ✓ When multiplying a monomial by a polynomial, use the distributive property.

$$a \times (b + c) = a \times b + a \times c = ab = ac$$

Examples:

1) Multiply expressions. $-4x(5x + 9) =$
   Use Distributive Property: $-4x(5x + 9) = -20x^2 - 36x$

2) Multiply expressions. $2x(6x^2 - 3y^2) =$
   Use Distributive Property: $2x(6x^2 - 3y^2) = 12x^3 - 6xy^2$

Multiplying Binomials

Step-by-step guide:

- ✓ Use "FOIL". (First-Out-In-Last)
$$(x + a)(x + b) = x^2 + (b + a)x + ab$$

Examples:

1) Multiply Binomials. $(x - 2)(x + 2) =$

   Use "FOIL". (First–Out–In–Last): $(x - 2)(x + 2) = x^2 + 2x - 2x - 4$

   Then simplify: $x^2 + 2x - 2x - 4 = x^2 - 4$

2) Multiply Binomials. $(x + 5)(x - 2) =$

   Use "FOIL". (First–Out–In–Last):

   $(x + 5)(x - 2) = x^2 - 2x + 5x - 10$

   Then simplify: $x^2 - 2x + 5x - 10 = x^2 + 3x - 10$

Factoring Trinomials

Step-by-step guide:

- ✓ "FOIL": $(x + a)(x + b) = x^2 + (b + a)x + ab$
- ✓ "Difference of Squares": $a^2 - b^2 = (a + b)(a - b)$
$$a^2 + 2ab + b^2 = (a + b)(a + b)$$
$$a^2 - 2ab + b^2 = (a - b)(a - b)$$
- ✓ "Reverse FOIL": $x^2 + (b + a)x + ab = (x + a)(x + b)$

Examples:

1) Factor this trinomial. $x^2 - 2x - 8 =$
   Break the expression into groups: $(x^2 + 2x) + (-4x - 8)$
   Now factor out x from $x^2 + 2x$: $x(x + 2)$ and factor out -4 from $-4x - 8$: $-4(x + 2)$
   Then: $= x(x + 2) - 4(x + 2)$, now factor out like term: $x + 2$
   Then: $(x + 2)(x - 4)$

2) Factor this trinomial. $x^2 - 6x + 8 =$
   Break the expression into groups: $(x^2 - 2x) + (-4x + 8)$
   Now factor out x from $x^2 - 2x$: $x(x - 2)$, and factor out -4 from $-4x + 8$: $-4(x - 2)$
   Then: $= x(x - 2) - 4(x - 2)$, now factor out like term: $x - 2$
   Then: $(x - 2)(x - 4)$

Operations with Polynomials

Step-by-step guide:

✓ When multiplying a monomial by a polynomial, use the distributive property.

$$a \times (b + c) = a \times b + a \times$$

Examples:

1) Multiply. $5(2x - 6) =$

   Use the distributive property: $5(2x - 6) = 10x - 30$

2) Multiply. $2x(6x + 2) =$

   Use the distributive property: $2x(6 + 2) = 12x^2 + 4x$

Day 6 Practices

✎ *Write each polynomial in standard form.*

1) $12x - 10x =$
2) $-3x - 3 + 14x - 11x =$
3) $5x^2 - 7x^3 =$
4) $3 + 4x^3 - 3 =$
5) $2x^2 + 1x - 6x^3 =$
6) $-x^2 + 2x^3 =$

✎ *Simplify each polynomial.*

7) $5(2x - 10) =$
8) $2x(4x - 2) =$
9) $4x(5x - 3) =$
10) $3x(7x + 3) =$
11) $4x(8x - 4) =$
12) $5x(5x + 4) =$

✎ *Add or subtract polynomials.*

13) $(-x^2 - 2) + (2x^2 + 1) =$
14) $(2x^2 + 3) - (3 - 4x^2) =$
15) $(2x^3 + 3x^2) - (x^3 + 8) =$
16) $(4x^3 - x^2) + (3x^2 - 5x) =$
17) $(7x^3 + 9x) - (3x^3 + 2) =$
18) $(2x^3 - 2) + (2x^3 + 2) =$

✎ *Simplify each expression. (Multiplying Monomials)*

19) $4u^7 \times (-2u^5) =$
20) $(-2p^7) \times (-3p^2) =$
21) $3xy^2z^3 \times 2z^2 =$
22) $5u^5t \times 3ut^2 =$
23) $(-9a^6) \times (-5a^2b^4) =$
24) $-2a^3b^2 \times 4a^2b =$

✎ *Simplify each expression. (Multiplying and Dividing Monomials)*

25) $(3x^7y^2)(16x^5y^4) =$
26) $(4x^4y^6)(7x^3y^4) =$
27) $(7x^2y^9)(12x^9y^{12}) =$
28) $\dfrac{12x^6y^8}{4x^4y^2} =$
29) $\dfrac{52x^9y^5}{4x^3y^4} =$
30) $\dfrac{80x^{12}y^9}{10x^6y^7} =$

✍ *Find each product. (Multiplying a Polynomial and a Monomial)*

31) $3x(9x + 2y) =$
32) $6x(x + 2y) =$
33) $9x(2x + 4y) =$

34) $12x(3x + 9) =$
35) $11x(2x - 11y) =$
36) $2x(6x - 6y) =$

✍ *Find each product. (Multiplying Binomials)*

37) $(x + 2)(x + 2) =$
38) $(x - 3)(x + 2) =$
39) $(x - 2)(x - 4) =$

40) $(x + 3)(x + 2) =$
41) $(x - 4)(x - 5) =$
42) $(x + 5)(x + 2) =$

✍ *Factor each trinomial.*

43) $x^2 + 8x + 15 =$
44) $x^2 - 5x + 6 =$
45) $x^2 + 6x + 8 =$

46) $x^2 - 8x + 16 =$
47) $x^2 - 7x + 12 =$
48) $x^2 + 11x + 18 =$

✍ *Find each product. (Operations with Polynomials)*

49) $9(6x + 2) =$
50) $8(3x + 7) =$
51) $5(6x - 1) =$

52) $-3(8x - 3) =$
53) $3x^2(6x - 5) =$
54) $5x^2(7x - 2) =$

Answers

1) $2x$
2) -3
3) $-7x^3 + 5x^2$
4) $4x^3$
5) $-6x^3 + 2x^2 + x$
6) $2x^3 - x^2$

7) $10x - 50$
8) $8x^2 - 4x$
9) $20x^2 - 12x$
10) $21x^2 + 9x$
11) $32x^2 - 16x$
12) $25x^2 + 20x$

13) $x^2 - 1$
14) $6x^2$
15) $x^3 + 3x^2 - 8$
16) $4x^3 + 2x^2 - 5x$
17) $4x^3 + 9x - 2$
18) $4x^3$

19) $-8u^{12}$
20) $6p^9$
21) $6xy^2z^5$
22) $15u^6t^3$
23) $45a^8b^4$
24) $-8a^5b^3$

25) $48x^{12}y^6$
26) $28x^7y^{10}$
27) $84x^{11}y^{21}$
28) $3x^2y^6$
29) $13x^6y$
30) $8x^6y^2$

31) $27x^2 + 6xy$
32) $6x^2 + 12xy$
33) $18x^2 + 36xy$
34) $36x^2 + 108x$
35) $22x^2 - 121xy$
36) $12x^2 - 12xy$

37) $x^2 + 4x + 4$
38) $x^2 - x - 6$
39) $x^2 - 6x + 8$
40) $x^2 + 5x + 6$
41) $x^2 - 9x + 20$
42) $x^2 + 7x + 10$

43) $(x + 3)(x + 5)$
44) $(x - 2)(x - 3)$
45) $(x + 4)(x + 2)$
46) $(x - 4)(x - 4)$
47) $(x - 3)(x - 4)$
48) $(x + 2)(x + 9)$

49) $54x + 18$
50) $24x + 56$
51) $30x - 5$
52) $-24x + 9$
53) $18x^3 - 15x^2$
54) $35x^3 - 10x^2$

Day 7:
Geometry and Statistics

Math Topics that you'll learn today:

- ✓ The Pythagorean Theorem
- ✓ Triangles
- ✓ Polygons
- ✓ Circles
- ✓ Trapezoids
- ✓ Cubes
- ✓ Rectangle Prisms
- ✓ Cylinder
- ✓ Mean, Median, Mode, and Range of the Given Data
- ✓ Bar Graph
- ✓ Box and Whisker Plots
- ✓ Stem– And– Leaf Plot
- ✓ Pie Graph
- ✓ Probability

Mathematics is like checkers in being suitable for the young, not too difficult, amusing, and without peril to the state. – Plato

The Pythagorean Theorem

Step-by-step guide:

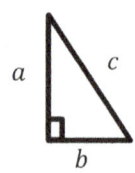

- ✓ In any right triangle: $a^2 + b^2 = c^2$

Examples:

1) Find the missing length.

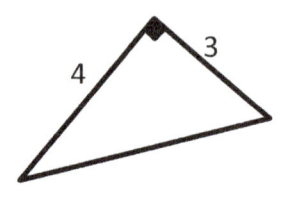

   Use Pythagorean Theorem: $a^2 + b^2 = c^2$

   Then: $a^2 + b^2 = c^2 \rightarrow 3^2 + 4^2 = c^2 \rightarrow 9 + 16 = c^2$

   $c^2 = 25 \rightarrow c = 5$

2) Right triangle ABC has two legs of lengths 6 cm (AB) and 8 cm (AC). What is the length of the third side (BC)?

   Use Pythagorean Theorem: $a^2 + b^2 = c^2$

   Then: $a^2 + b^2 = c^2 \rightarrow 6^2 + 8^2 = c^2 \rightarrow 36 + 64 = c^2$

   $c^2 = 100 \rightarrow c = 10$

Triangles

Step-by-step guide:

- ✓ In any triangle the sum of all angles is 180 degrees.
- ✓ Area of a triangle = $\frac{1}{2}$ (base × height)

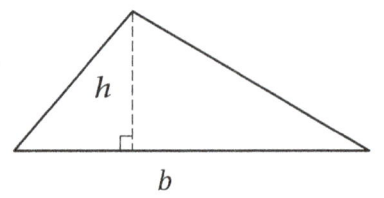

Examples:

What is the area of triangles?

1)

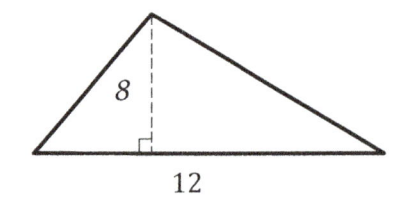

Solution:
Use the are formula: Area = $\frac{1}{2}$ (base × height)
base = 12 and height = 8
Area = $\frac{1}{2}(12 \times 8) = \frac{1}{2}(96) = 48$

2)

Solution:
Use the are formula: Area = $\frac{1}{2}$ (base × height)
base = 6 and height = 5
Area = $\frac{1}{2}(5 \times 6) = \frac{30}{2} = 15$

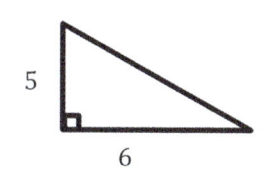

Polygons

Step-by-step guide:

Perimeter of a square = $4 \times side = 4s$

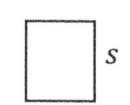

Perimeter of a rectangle = $2(width + length)$

Perimeter of trapezoid = $a + b + c + d$

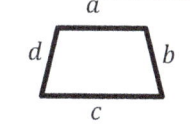

Perimeter of a regular hexagon = $6a$

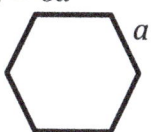

Example: Find the perimeter of following regular hexagon.

Perimeter of Pentagon = $6a$

Perimeter of Pentagon = $6a = 6 \times 3 = 18m$

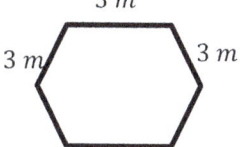

Perimeter of a parallelogram = $2(l + w)$

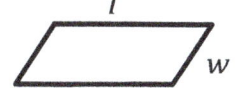

Circles

Step-by-step guide:

- In a circle, variable r is usually used for the radius and d for diameter and π is about 3.14.
- Area of a circle = πr^2
- Circumference of a circle = $2\pi r$

Examples:

1) Find the area of the circle.
   Use area formula: Area = πr^2,
   $r = 4$ then: Area = $\pi(4)^2 = 16\pi$, $\pi = 3.14$ then:
   Area = $16 \times 3.14 = 50.24$

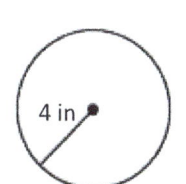

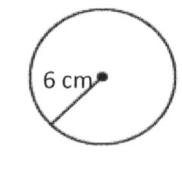

2) Find the Circumference of the circle.
   Use Circumference formula: $Circumference = 2\pi r$
   $r = 6$, then: $Circumference = 2\pi(6) = 12\pi$
   $\pi = 3.14$ then: $Circumference = 12 \times 3.14 = 37.68$
   $(\pi = 3.14)$

Trapezoids

Step-by-step guide:

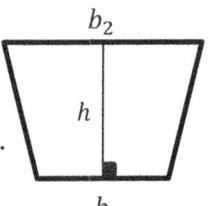

- ✓ A quadrilateral with at least one pair of parallel sides is a trapezoid.
- ✓ Area of a trapezoid $= \frac{1}{2}h(b_1 + b_2)$

Example:

Calculate the area of the trapezoid.

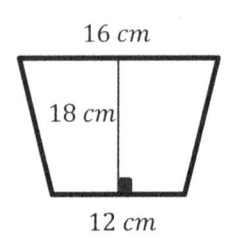

Use area formula: $A = \frac{1}{2}h(b_1 + b_2)$

$b_1 = 12$, $b_2 = 16$ and $h = 18$

Then: $A = \frac{1}{2}18(12 + 16) = 9(28) = 252\ cm^2$

Cubes

Step-by-step guide:

- ✓ A cube is a three-dimensional solid object bounded by six square sides.
- ✓ Volume is the measure of the amount of space inside of a solid figure, like a cube, ball, cylinder or pyramid.
- ✓ Volume of a cube $= (one\ side)^3$
- ✓ surface area of cube $= 6 \times (one\ side)^2$

Example:

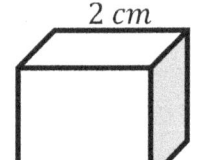

Find the volume and surface area of this cube.

Use volume formula: $volume = (one\ side)^3$

Then: $volume = (one\ side)^3 = (2)^3 = 8\ cm^3$

Use surface area formula: $surface\ area\ of\ cube: 6(one\ side)^2 = 6(2)^2 = 6(4) = 24\ cm^2$

Rectangular Prisms

Step-by-step guide:

- ✓ A solid 3-dimensional object which has six rectangular faces.
- ✓ Volume of a Rectangular prism = **Length × Width × Height**

$Volume = l \times w \times h$ $Surface\ area = 2(wh + lw + lh)$

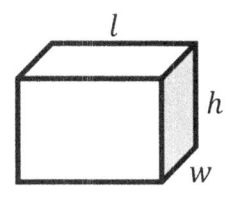

Example:

Find the volume and surface area of rectangular prism.

Use volume formula: $Volume = l \times w \times h$

Then: $Volume = 10 \times 5 \times 8 = 400\ m^3$

Use surface area formula: $Surface\ area = 2(wh + lw + lh)$

Then: $Surface\ area = 2(5 \times 8 + 10 \times 5 + 10 \times 8) = 2(40 + 50 + 80) = 340\ m^2$

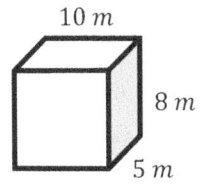

Cylinder

Step-by-step guide:

- ✓ A cylinder is a solid geometric figure with straight parallel sides and a circular or oval cross section.
- ✓ $Volume\ of\ Cylinder\ Formula = \pi(radius)^2 \times height\ (\pi = 3.14)$
- ✓ $Surface\ area\ of\ a\ cylinder = 2\pi r^2 + 2\pi rh$

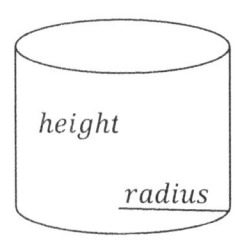

Example:

Find the volume and Surface area of the follow Cylinder.

Use volume formula: $Volume = \pi(radius)^2 \times height$
Then: $Volume = \pi(4)^2 \times 6 = \pi 16 \times 6 = 96\pi$
$\pi = 3.14$ then: $Volume = 96\pi = 301.44$
Use surface area formula: $Surface\ area = 2\pi r^2 + 2\pi rh$
Then: $= 2\pi(4)^2 + 2\pi(4)(6) = 2\pi(16) + 2\pi(24) = 32\pi + 48\pi = 80\pi$
$\pi = 3.14$ then: $Surface\ area = 80 \times 3.14 = 251.2$

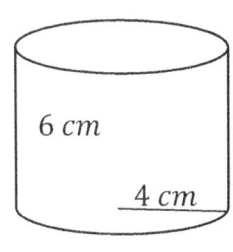

Mean, Median, Mode, and Range of the Given Data

Step-by-step guide:

- ✓ Mean: $\dfrac{\text{sum of the data}}{\text{total number of data entires}}$
- ✓ Mode: value in the list that appears most often
- ✓ Range: the difference of largest value and smallest value in the list

Examples:

1) What is the median of these numbers? 4, 9, 13, 8, 15, 18, 5

   Write the numbers in order: 4, 5, 8, 9, 13, 15, 18

   Median is the number in the middle. Therefore, the median is 9.

2) What is the mode of these numbers? 22, 16, 12, 9, 7, 6, 4, 6

   Mode: value in the list that appears most often
   Therefore: mode is 6

Pie Graph

Step-by-step guide:

- ✓ A Pie Chart is a circle chart divided into sectors, each sector represents the relative size of each value.

Example:

A library has 840 books that include Mathematics, Physics, Chemistry, English and History. Use following graph to answer question.

What is the number of Mathematics books?

Number of total books = 840,
Percent of Mathematics books = 30% = 0.30
Then: 0.30 × 840 = 252

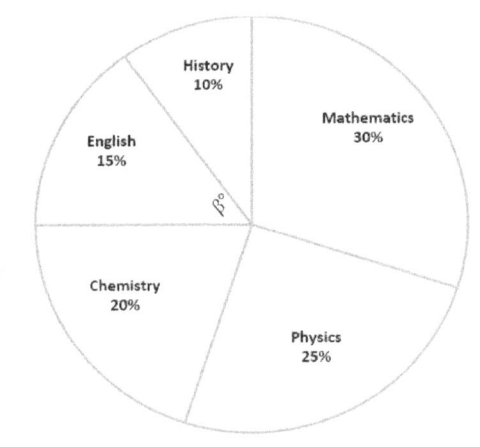

74

Probability Problems

Step-by-step guide:

- ✓ Probability is the likelihood of something happening in the future. It is expressed as a number between zero (can never happen) to 1 (will always happen).
- ✓ Probability can be expressed as a fraction, a decimal, or a percent.

Examples:

1) If there are 8 red balls and 12 blue balls in a basket, what is the probability that John will pick out a red ball from the basket?

   There are 8 red ball and 20 are total number of balls. Therefore, probability that John will pick out a red ball from the basket is 8 out of 20 or $\frac{8}{8+12} = \frac{8}{20} = \frac{2}{5}$.

2) A bag contains 18 balls: two green, five black, eight blue, a brown, a red and one white. If 17 balls are removed from the bag at random, what is the probability that a brown ball has been removed?

   If 17 balls are removed from the bag at random, there will be one ball in the bag.
   The probability of choosing a brown ball is 1 out of 18. Therefore, the probability of not choosing a brown ball is 17 out of 18 and the probability of having not a brown ball after removing 17 balls is the same.

Prepare for the ASVAB Math Test in 7 Days

Day 7 Practices

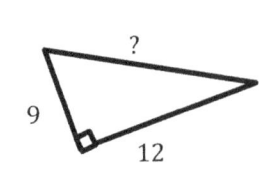

✏️ **Find the missing side?**

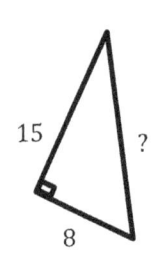

1) Triangle with legs 3 and 4, hypotenuse ?

2) Right triangle with sides 15, 8, hypotenuse ?

3) Right triangle with legs 9 and 12, hypotenuse ?

4) Right triangle with leg 6, hypotenuse 10, other leg ?

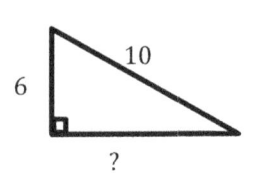

✏️ **Find the measure of the unknown angle in each triangle.**

5) Triangle with angles 70°, 95°, ?°

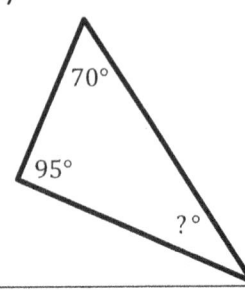

6) Triangle with angles 60°, 85°, ?°

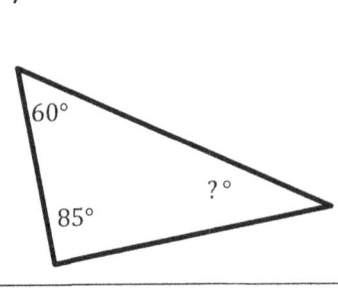

7) Triangle with angles 80°, 85°, ?°

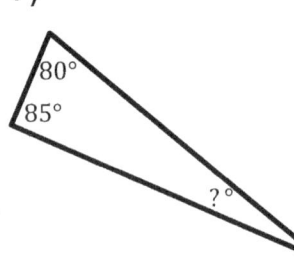

8) Triangle with angles 50°, 65°, ?°

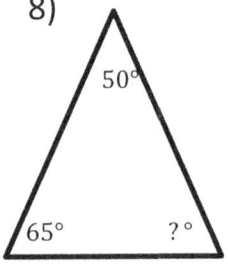

✏️ **Find the perimeter of each shape.**

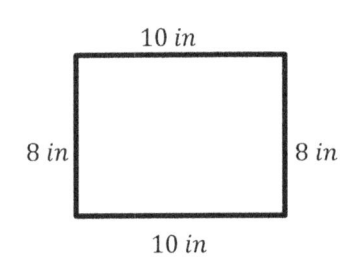

9) Rhombus with all sides 12 ft

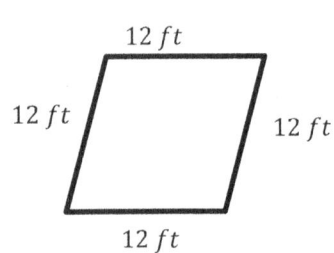

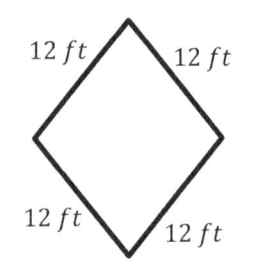

10) Rectangle 10 in by 8 in

11) Rhombus with all sides 12 ft

12) Square with side 14 cm

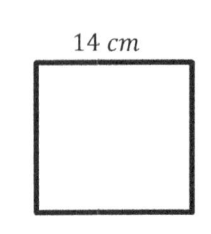

✏️ **Complete the table below.** (π = 3.14)

13)

	Radius	Diameter	Circumference	Area
Circle 1	4 inches	8 inches	25.12 inches	50.24 square inches
Circle 2		12 meters		
Circle 3				12.56 square ft
Circle 4			18.84 miles	

Find the area of each trapezoid.

14) 9 cm (top), 6 cm (left), 12 cm (bottom)

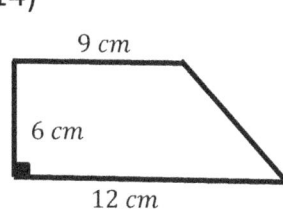

15) 14 m (top), 10 m (height), 18 m (bottom)

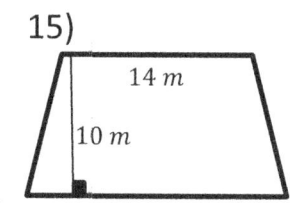

16) 5 ft (top), 4 ft (height), 7 ft (bottom)

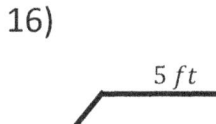

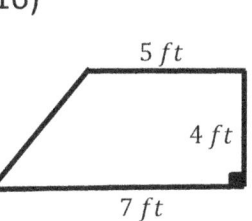

17) 7 cm (top), 5 cm (height), 10 cm (bottom)

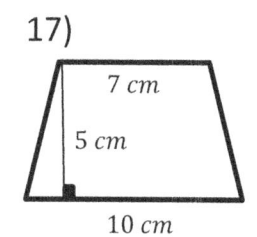

Find the volume of each cube.

18) 4 ft

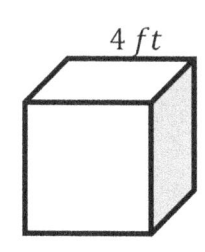

19) 6 m

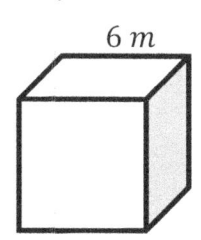

20) 1 in

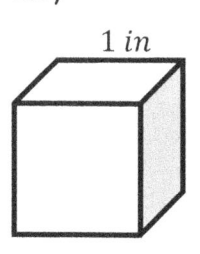

21) 3 miles

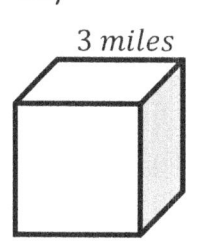

Find the volume of each Rectangular Prism.

22) 7 m, 6 m, 5 m

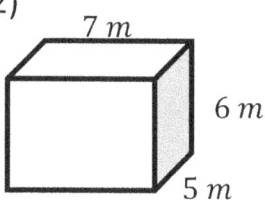

23) 10 in, 8 in, 4 in

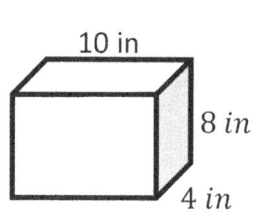

24) 9 m, 7 m, 3 m

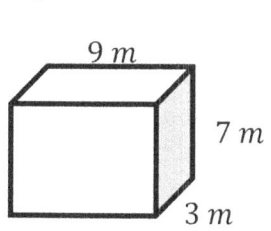

Find the volume of each Cylinder. Round your answer to the nearest tenth. (π = 3.14)

25) 8 m, 10 m

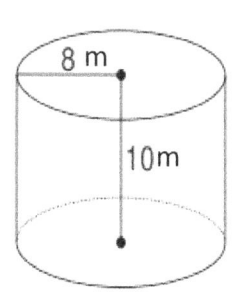

26) 2 cm, 4 cm

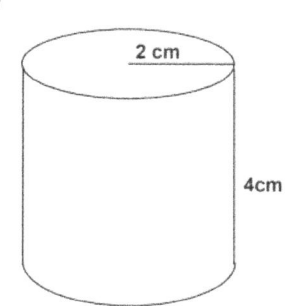

27) 6 cm, 5 cm

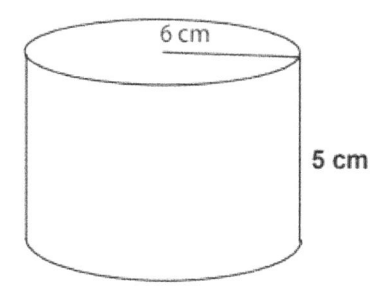

✍ **Solve.**

28) In a javelin throw competition, five athletics score 56, 58, 63, 57 and 61 meters. What are their Mean and Median? _____

✍ The circle graph below shows all Jason's expenses for last month. Jason spent $300 on his bills last month.

29) How much did Jason spend on his car last month? _____

30) How much did Jason spend for foods last month? _____

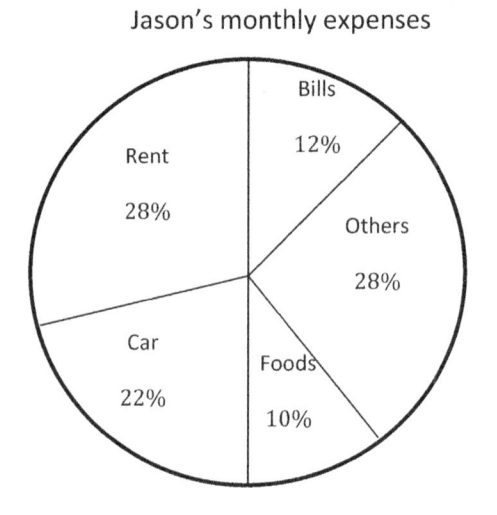

Jason's monthly expenses

- Bills 12%
- Others 28%
- Foods 10%
- Car 22%
- Rent 28%

Solve.

31) Bag A contains 9 red marbles and 3 green marbles. Bag B contains 9 black marbles and 6 orange marbles. What is the probability of selecting a green marble at random from bag A? What is the probability of selecting a black marble at random from Bag B? _____ _____

Answers

1) 5
2) 17
3) 15
4) 8

5) 15°
6) 35°
7) 15°
8) 65°

9) 48 ft
10) 36 in
11) 48 ft
12) 56 cm

13)

	Radius	Diameter	Circumference	Area
Circle 1	4 inches	8 inches	25.12 inches	50.24 square inches
Circle 2	6 meters	12 meters	37.68 meters	113.04 meters
Circle 3	2 square ft	4 square ft	12.56 square ft	12.56 square ft
Circle 4	3 miles	6 miles	18.84 miles	28.26 miles

14) 63 cm^2
15) 160 m^2
16) 24 ft^2
17) 42.5 cm^2

18) 64 ft^3
19) 216 m^3
20) 1 in^3
21) 27 $miles^3$

22) 210 m^3
23) 320 in^3
24) 189 m^3

25) 2,009.6 m^3
26) 50.24 cm^3
27) 565.2 cm^3
28) Mean: 59, Median: 58
29) $550
30) $250
31) $\frac{1}{4}, \frac{3}{5}$

AFOQT Test Review

The Armed Services Vocational Aptitude Battery (ASVAB) was introduced in 1968. Over 40 million examinees have taken the AFOQT since then.

According to official AFOQT website, the AFOQT is a multiple-aptitude battery that measures developed abilities and helps predict future academic and occupational success in the military. It is administered annually to more than one million military applicants, high school, and post-secondary students.

AFOQT scores are reported as percentiles between 1-99. An AFOQT percentile score indicates the percentage of examinees in a reference group that scored at or below that particular score. For example, AFOQT score of 90 indicates that the examinee scored as well as or better than 90% of the nationally-representative sample test takers. An AFOQT score of 60 indicates that the examinee scored as well as or better than 60% of the nationally-representative sample.

There are three types of ASVAB:

- The CAT-AFOQT (computer adaptive test)
- The MET-site AFOQT (paper and pencil (P&P)
- The Student AFOQT (paper and pencil (P&P)

The CAT-AFOQT is a computer adaptive test. It means that if the correct answer is chosen, the next question will be harder. If the answer given is incorrect, the next question will be easier. This also means that once an answer is selected on the CAT it cannot be changed.

The MET- site AFOQT and The Student AFOQT are paper and pencil (P&P) tests.

In this section, there are 2 complete Arithmetic Reasoning and Mathematics Knowledge AFOQT Tests. There is a complete test for CAT-AFOQT and another complete test for paper and pencil (P&P). Take these tests to see what score you'll be able to receive on a real AFOQT test.

Good luck!

Prepare for the ASVAB Math Test in 7 Days

AFOQT Math Practice Tests

Time to Test

Time to refine your Math skill with a practice test

In this section, there are two complete AFOQT Mathematics practice tests, one computer based (CAT-ASVAB) and one Paper and Pencil test. Take these tests to simulate the test day experience. After you've finished, score your tests using the answer keys.

Before You Start

- You'll need a pencil and a timer to take the test.
- For each question, there are four possible answers. Choose which one is best.
- It's okay to guess. There is no penalty for wrong answers.
- Use the answer sheet provided to record your answers.
- After you've finished the test, review the answer key to see where you went wrong.

Calculators are NOT permitted for the AFOQT Test

Good Luck!

Mathematics is like love; a simple idea, but it can get complicated.

AFOQT Math Practice Test 1 Answer Sheet

Remove (or photocopy) this answer sheet and use it to complete the practice test.

AFOQT Math Practice Test 1 (CAT-ASVAB) Answer Sheet

AFOQT Practice Test 1 — Arithmetic Reasoning

1	Ⓐ Ⓑ Ⓒ Ⓓ Ⓔ	11	Ⓐ Ⓑ Ⓒ Ⓓ Ⓔ
2	Ⓐ Ⓑ Ⓒ Ⓓ Ⓔ	12	Ⓐ Ⓑ Ⓒ Ⓓ Ⓔ
3	Ⓐ Ⓑ Ⓒ Ⓓ Ⓔ	13	Ⓐ Ⓑ Ⓒ Ⓓ Ⓔ
4	Ⓐ Ⓑ Ⓒ Ⓓ Ⓔ	14	Ⓐ Ⓑ Ⓒ Ⓓ Ⓔ
5	Ⓐ Ⓑ Ⓒ Ⓓ Ⓔ	15	Ⓐ Ⓑ Ⓒ Ⓓ Ⓔ
6	Ⓐ Ⓑ Ⓒ Ⓓ Ⓔ	16	Ⓐ Ⓑ Ⓒ Ⓓ Ⓔ
7	Ⓐ Ⓑ Ⓒ Ⓓ Ⓔ	17	
8	Ⓐ Ⓑ Ⓒ Ⓓ Ⓔ	18	
9	Ⓐ Ⓑ Ⓒ Ⓓ Ⓔ	19	
10	Ⓐ Ⓑ Ⓒ Ⓓ Ⓔ	20	

AFOQT Practice Test 1 — Mathematics Knowledge

1	Ⓐ Ⓑ Ⓒ Ⓓ Ⓔ	11	Ⓐ Ⓑ Ⓒ Ⓓ Ⓔ
2	Ⓐ Ⓑ Ⓒ Ⓓ Ⓔ	12	Ⓐ Ⓑ Ⓒ Ⓓ Ⓔ
3	Ⓐ Ⓑ Ⓒ Ⓓ Ⓔ	13	Ⓐ Ⓑ Ⓒ Ⓓ Ⓔ
4	Ⓐ Ⓑ Ⓒ Ⓓ Ⓔ	14	Ⓐ Ⓑ Ⓒ Ⓓ Ⓔ
5	Ⓐ Ⓑ Ⓒ Ⓓ Ⓔ	15	Ⓐ Ⓑ Ⓒ Ⓓ Ⓔ
6	Ⓐ Ⓑ Ⓒ Ⓓ Ⓔ	16	Ⓐ Ⓑ Ⓒ Ⓓ Ⓔ
7	Ⓐ Ⓑ Ⓒ Ⓓ Ⓔ		
8	Ⓐ Ⓑ Ⓒ Ⓓ Ⓔ		
9	Ⓐ Ⓑ Ⓒ Ⓓ Ⓔ		
10	Ⓐ Ⓑ Ⓒ Ⓓ Ⓔ		

AFOQT Math Practice Test 2 (Paper and Pencil) Answer Sheet

AFOQT Practice Test 2 — Arithmetic Reasoning

1	Ⓐ Ⓑ Ⓒ Ⓓ Ⓔ	11	Ⓐ Ⓑ Ⓒ Ⓓ Ⓔ	21	Ⓐ Ⓑ Ⓒ Ⓓ Ⓔ
2	Ⓐ Ⓑ Ⓒ Ⓓ Ⓔ	12	Ⓐ Ⓑ Ⓒ Ⓓ Ⓔ	22	Ⓐ Ⓑ Ⓒ Ⓓ Ⓔ
3	Ⓐ Ⓑ Ⓒ Ⓓ Ⓔ	13	Ⓐ Ⓑ Ⓒ Ⓓ Ⓔ	23	Ⓐ Ⓑ Ⓒ Ⓓ Ⓔ
4	Ⓐ Ⓑ Ⓒ Ⓓ Ⓔ	14	Ⓐ Ⓑ Ⓒ Ⓓ Ⓔ	24	Ⓐ Ⓑ Ⓒ Ⓓ Ⓔ
5	Ⓐ Ⓑ Ⓒ Ⓓ Ⓔ	15	Ⓐ Ⓑ Ⓒ Ⓓ Ⓔ	25	Ⓐ Ⓑ Ⓒ Ⓓ Ⓔ
6	Ⓐ Ⓑ Ⓒ Ⓓ Ⓔ	16	Ⓐ Ⓑ Ⓒ Ⓓ Ⓔ	26	Ⓐ Ⓑ Ⓒ Ⓓ Ⓔ
7	Ⓐ Ⓑ Ⓒ Ⓓ Ⓔ	17	Ⓐ Ⓑ Ⓒ Ⓓ Ⓔ	27	Ⓐ Ⓑ Ⓒ Ⓓ Ⓔ
8	Ⓐ Ⓑ Ⓒ Ⓓ Ⓔ	18	Ⓐ Ⓑ Ⓒ Ⓓ Ⓔ	28	Ⓐ Ⓑ Ⓒ Ⓓ Ⓔ
9	Ⓐ Ⓑ Ⓒ Ⓓ Ⓔ	19	Ⓐ Ⓑ Ⓒ Ⓓ Ⓔ	29	Ⓐ Ⓑ Ⓒ Ⓓ Ⓔ
10	Ⓐ Ⓑ Ⓒ Ⓓ Ⓔ	20	Ⓐ Ⓑ Ⓒ Ⓓ Ⓔ	30	Ⓐ Ⓑ Ⓒ Ⓓ Ⓔ

AFOQT Practice Test 2 — Mathematics Knowledge

1	Ⓐ Ⓑ Ⓒ Ⓓ Ⓔ	11	Ⓐ Ⓑ Ⓒ Ⓓ Ⓔ	21	Ⓐ Ⓑ Ⓒ Ⓓ Ⓔ
2	Ⓐ Ⓑ Ⓒ Ⓓ Ⓔ	12	Ⓐ Ⓑ Ⓒ Ⓓ Ⓔ	22	Ⓐ Ⓑ Ⓒ Ⓓ Ⓔ
3	Ⓐ Ⓑ Ⓒ Ⓓ Ⓔ	13	Ⓐ Ⓑ Ⓒ Ⓓ Ⓔ	23	Ⓐ Ⓑ Ⓒ Ⓓ Ⓔ
4	Ⓐ Ⓑ Ⓒ Ⓓ Ⓔ	14	Ⓐ Ⓑ Ⓒ Ⓓ Ⓔ	24	Ⓐ Ⓑ Ⓒ Ⓓ Ⓔ
5	Ⓐ Ⓑ Ⓒ Ⓓ Ⓔ	15	Ⓐ Ⓑ Ⓒ Ⓓ Ⓔ	25	Ⓐ Ⓑ Ⓒ Ⓓ Ⓔ
6	Ⓐ Ⓑ Ⓒ Ⓓ Ⓔ	16	Ⓐ Ⓑ Ⓒ Ⓓ Ⓔ		
7	Ⓐ Ⓑ Ⓒ Ⓓ Ⓔ	17	Ⓐ Ⓑ Ⓒ Ⓓ Ⓔ		
8	Ⓐ Ⓑ Ⓒ Ⓓ Ⓔ	18	Ⓐ Ⓑ Ⓒ Ⓓ Ⓔ		
9	Ⓐ Ⓑ Ⓒ Ⓓ Ⓔ	19	Ⓐ Ⓑ Ⓒ Ⓓ Ⓔ		
10	Ⓐ Ⓑ Ⓒ Ⓓ Ⓔ	20	Ⓐ Ⓑ Ⓒ Ⓓ Ⓔ		

AFOQT Math Practice Test 1 CAT-AFOQT Arithmetic Reasoning

- **16 questions**
- **Total time for this section:** 39 Minutes
- **Calculators are not allowed for this test.**

1) Aria was hired to teach three identical math courses, which entailed being present in the classroom 36 hours altogether. At $25 per class hour, how much did Aria earn for teaching one course?

   A. $50

   B. $300

   C. $600

   D. $1,400

2) Karen is 9 years older than her sister Michelle, and Michelle is 4 years younger than her brother David. If the sum of their ages is 82, how old is Michelle?

   A. 21

   B. 25

   C. 29

   D. 23

3) John is driving to visit his mother, who lives 300 miles away. How long will the drive be, round-trip, if John drives at an average speed of 50 mph?

   A. 95 Minutes

   B. 260 Minutes

   C. 645 Minutes

   D. 720 Minutes

4) Julie gives 8 pieces of candy to each of her friends. If Julie gives all her candy away, which amount of candy could have been the amount she distributed?

   A. 187

   B. 216

   C. 343

   D. 223

5) If a rectangle is 30 feet by 45 feet, what is its area?

   A. 1,350

   B. 1,250

   C. 1,000

   D. 750

6) You are asked to chart the temperature during an 8 hour period to give the average. These are your results:

   7 am: 2 degrees   11 am: 32 degrees

   8 am: 5 degrees   12 pm: 35 degrees

   9 am: 22 degrees   1 pm: 35 degrees

   10 am: 28 degrees   2 pm: 33 degrees

   What is the average temperature?

   A. 36   C. 24

   B. 28   D. 22

7) Each year, a cyber café charges its customers a base rate of $15, with an additional $0.20 per visit for the first 40 visits, and $0.10 for every visit after that. How much does the cyber café charge a customer for a year in which 60 visits are made?

   A. $25   C. $35

   B. $29   D. $39

8) If a vehicle is driven 32 miles on Monday, 35 miles on Tuesday, and 29 miles on Wednesday, what is the average number of miles driven each day?

   A. 32 Miles   C. 29 Miles

   B. 31 Miles   D. 27 Miles

9) Three co-workers contributed $10.25, $11.25, and $18.45 respectively to purchase a retirement gift for their boss. What is the maximum amount they can spend on a gift?

   A. $42.25   C. $39.95

   B. $40.17   D. $27.06

10) While at work, Emma checks her email once every 90 minutes. In 9-hour, how many times does she check her email?

   A. 4 Times

   B. 5 Times

   C. 7 Times

   D. 6 Times

11) A family owns 15 dozen of magazines. After donating 57 magazines to the public library, how many magazines are still with the family?

   A. 180

   B. 152

   C. 123

   D. 98

12) In the deck of cards, there are 4 spades, 3 hearts, 7 clubs, and 10 diamonds. What is the probability that William will pick out a spade?

   A. 1/6

   B. 1/8

   C. 1/9

   D. 1/5

13) What is the prime factorization of 560?

   A. $2 \times 2 \times 5 \times 7$

   B. $2 \times 2 \times 2 \times 2 \times 5 \times 7$

   C. 2×7

   D. $2 \times 2 \times 2 \times 5 \times 7$

14) William is driving a truck that can hold 5 tons maximum. He has a shipment of food weighing 32,000 pounds. How many trips will he need to make to deliver all of the food?

   A. 1 Trip

   B. 3 Trips

   C. 4 Trips

   D. 6 Trips

15) A man goes to a casino with $180. He loses $40 on blackjack, then loses another $50 on roulette. How much money does he have left?

    A. $75

    B. $90

    C. $105

    D. $120

16) A woman owns a dog walking business. If 3 workers can walk 9 dogs, how many dogs can 5 workers walk?

    A. 13

    B. 14

    C. 15

    D. 19

IF YOU FINISH BEFORE TIME IS CALLED, YOU MAY CHECK YOUR WORK ON THIS SECTION ONLY. DO NOT TURN TO OTHER SECTION IN THE TEST.

STOP

AFOQT Math Practice Test 1 CAT-AFOQT Mathematics Knowledge

- **Total time for this section:** 18 Minutes
- **16 questions**
- **Calculators are not allowed for this test.**

1) If a = 3, what is the value of b in this equation?

$$b = \frac{a^2}{3} + 3$$

    A. 10   C. 6

    B. 8   D. 4

2) The eighth root of 256 is:

    A. 6   C. 8

    B. 4   D. 2

3) A circle has a radius of 5 inches. What is its approximate area? (π = 3.14)

    A. 90.7 square inches   C. 31.4 square inches

    B. 78.5 square inches   D. 25 square inches

4) If $-8a = 64$, then $a =$ ___

    A. −8   C. 16

    B. 8   D. 0

5) In the following diagram what is the value of x?

    A. 60°

    B. 90°

    C. 45°

    D. 15°

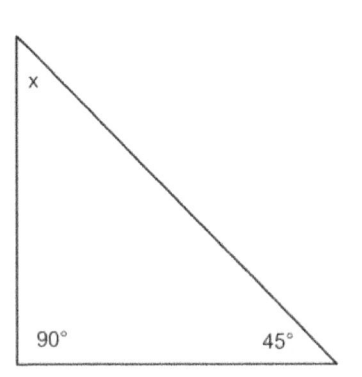

6) In the following right triangle, what is the value of x rounded to the nearest hundredth?

   A. 23.24

   B. 2.33

   C. 10.29

   D. 6.40

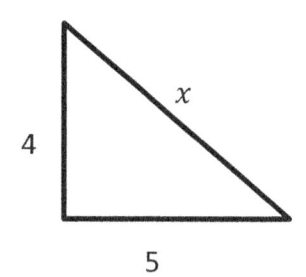

7) $(5x + 5)(2x + 6) = ?$

   A. $5x + 6$

   B. $10x^2 + 40x + 30$

   C. $5x + 5x + 30$

   D. $5x^2 + 5$

8) $5(a - 6) = 22$, what is the value of a?

   A. 2.4

   B. 10.4

   C. 7

   D. 11

9) If $3^{24} = 3^8 \times 3^x$, what is the value of x?

   A. 2

   B. 1.5

   C. 3

   D. 16

10) Which of the following is an obtuse angle?

    A. 116°

    B. 80°

    C. 68°

    D. 25°

11) Factor this expression: $x^2 + 5 - 6$

A. $x^2(5 + 6)$

B. $x(x + 5 - 6)$

C. $(x + 6)(x - 1)$

D. $(x + 6)(x - 6)$

12) Find the slope of the line running through the points (6, 7) and (5, 3).

A. $\dfrac{1}{4}$

B. 4

C. -4

D. $-\dfrac{1}{4}$

13) What is the value of $\sqrt{100} \times \sqrt{36}$?

A. 120

B. $\sqrt{136}$

C. 60

D. $\sqrt{16}$

14) Which of the following is not equal to 5^2?

A. the square of 5

B. 5 squared

C. 5 cubed

D. 5 to the second power

15) The cube root of 2,197 is?

A. 133

B. 13

C. 6.5

D. 169

16) What is 952,710 in scientific notation?

A. 95.271

B. 9.5271×10^5

C. 0.095271×10^6

D. 0.95271

5) During the last week of track training, Emma achieves the following times in seconds: 66, 57, 54, 64, 57, and 59. Her three best times this week (least times) are averaged for her final score on the course. What is her final score?

   A. 56 seconds

   B. 57 seconds

   C. 59 seconds

   D. 61 seconds

6) How many square feet of tile is needed for a 15 feet x 15 feet room?

   A. 225 square feet

   B. 118.5 square feet

   C. 112 square feet

   D. 60 square feet

7) With what number must 1.303572 be multiplied in order to obtain the number 1303.572?

   A. 100

   B. 1,000

   C. 10,000

   D. 100,000

8) Which of the following is NOT a factor of 50?

   A. 5

   B. 2

   C. 10

   D. 15

9) Emma is working in a hospital supply room and makes $25.00 an hour. The union negotiates a new contract giving each employee a 4% cost of living raise. What is Emma's new hourly rate?

   A. $26 an hour

   B. $28 an hour

   C. $30 an hour

   D. $31.50 an hour

10) Emily and Lucas have taken the same number of photos on their school trip. Emily has taken 4 times as many photos as Mia. Lucas has taken 21 more photos than Mia. How many photos has Mia taken?

   A. 7

   B. 9

   C. 11

   D. 13

11) Will has been working on a report for 5 hours each day, 6 days a week for 2 weeks. How many minutes has Will worked on his report?

   A. 7,444 minutes

   B. 5,524 minutes

   C. 3,600 minutes

   D. 2,640 minutes

12) Find the average of the following numbers: 22, 34, 16, 20

   A. 23

   B. 35

   C. 30

   D. 23.3

13) A mobile classroom is a rectangular block that is 90 feet by 30 feet in length and width respectively. If a student walks around the block once, how many yards does the student cover?

   A. 2,700 yards

   B. 240 yards

   C. 120 yards

   D. 60 yards

14) What is the distance in miles of a trip that takes 2.1 hours at an average speed of 16.2 miles per hour? (Round your answer to a whole number)

   A. 44 miles

   B. 34 miles

   C. 30 miles

   D. 18 miles

15) The sum of 6 numbers is greater than 120 and less than 180. Which of the following could be the average (arithmetic mean) of the numbers?

   A. 20

   B. 26

   C. 30

   D. 34

16) A barista averages making 15 coffees per hour. At this rate, how many hours will it take until she's made 1,500 coffees?

   A. 95 hours

   B. 90 hours

   C. 100 hours

   D. 105 hours

17) There are 120 rooms that need to be painted and only 12 painters available. If there are still 12 rooms unpainted by the end of the day, what is the average number of rooms that each painter has painted?

   A. 9

   B. 12

   C. 14

   D. 16

18) Nicole was making $7.50 per hour and got a raise to $7.75 per hour. What percentage increase was Nicole's raise?

   A. 2%

   B. 1.67%

   C. 3.33%

   D. 6.66%

19) An architect's floor plan uses ½ inch to represent one mile. What is the actual distance represented by 4 ½ inches?

   A. 9 miles

   B. 8 miles

   C. 7 miles

   D. 6 miles

20) A snack machine accepts only quarters. Candy bars cost 25¢, a package of peanuts costs 75¢, and a can of cola costs 50¢. How many quarters are needed to buy two Candy bars, one package of peanuts, and one can of cola?

   A. 8 quarters

   B. 7 quarters

   C. 6 quarters

   D. 5 quarters

21) The hour hand of a watch rotates 30 degrees every hour. How many complete rotations does the hour hand make in 8 days?

   A. 12

   B. 14

   C. 16

   D. 18

22) What is the product of the square root of 81 and the square root of 25?

   A. 2,025

   B. 15

   C. 25

   D. 45

23) If $2y + 4y + 2y = -24$, then what is the value of y?

   A. −3

   B. −2

   C. −1

   D. 0

24) A bread recipe calls for $2\frac{2}{3}$ cups of flour. If you only have $1\frac{5}{6}$ cups of flour, how much more flour is needed?

   A. 1

   B. $\frac{1}{2}$

   C. 2

   D. $\frac{5}{6}$

25) Convert 0.023 to a percent.

   A. 0.2%

   B. 0.23%

   C. 2.30%

   D. 23%

26) Will has been working on a report for 3 hours each day, 7 days a week for 2 weeks. How many minutes has will worked on his report?

   A. 6,364 minutes

   B. 4,444 minutes

   C. 2,520 minutes

   D. 1560 minutes

27) A writer finishes 180 pages of his manuscript in 20 hours. How many pages is his average per hour?

   A. 18

   B. 6

   C. 3

   D. 9

28) Camille uses a 30% off coupon when buying a sweater that costs $50. If she also pays 5% sales tax on the purchase, how much does she pay?

   A. $35

   B. $36.75

   C. $39.95

   D. $47.17

29) I've got 34 quarts of milk and my family drinks 2 gallons of milk per week. How many weeks will that last us?

   A. 2 weeks

   B. 2.5 weeks

   C. 3.25 weeks

   D. 4.25 weeks

30) A floppy disk shows 937,036 bytes free and 739,352 bytes used. If you delete a file of size 652,159 bytes and create a new file of size 599,986 bytes, how many free bytes will the floppy disk have?

A. 687,179

B. 791,525

C. 884,867

D. 989,209

AFOQT Math Practice Test 2

Paper and Pencil-AFOQT

Mathematics Knowledge

- 25 questions
- **Total time for this section:** 24 Minutes
- **Calculators are not allowed for this test.**

1) $(x + 7)(x + 5) = ?$

   A. $x^2 + 12x + 12$

   B. $2x + 12x + 12$

   C. $x^2 + 35x + 12$

   D. $x^2 + 12x + 35$

2) Convert 670,000 to scientific notation.

   A. 6.70×1000

   B. 6.70×10^{-5}

   C. 6.70×100

   D. 6.7×10^5

3) What is the perimeter of the triangle in the provided diagram?

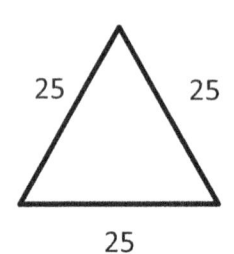

   A. 15,625

   B. 625

   C. 75

   D. 25

4) If x is a positive integer divisible by 6, and $x < 60$, what is the greatest possible value of x?

   A. 54

   B. 48

   C. 36

   D. 59

5) There are two pizza ovens in a restaurant. Oven 1 burns four times as many pizzas as oven 2. If the restaurant had a total of 15 burnt pizzas on Saturday, how many pizzas did oven 2 burn?

   A. 3

   B. 6

   C. 9

   D. 12

6) Which of the following is an obtuse angle?

   A. 56°

   B. 72°

   C. 123°

   D. 211°

7) $7^7 \times 7^8 = ?$

   A. 7^{56}

   B. $7^{0.89}$

   C. 7^{15}

   D. 1^7

8) What is 5231.48245 rounded to the nearest tenth?

   A. 5231.482

   B. 5231.5

   C. 5231

   D. 5231.48

9) The cube root of 512 is?

   A. 8

   B. 88

   C. 888

   D. 134,217,728

10) A circle has a diameter of 16 inches. What is its approximate area? (π = 3.14)

    A. 200.96

    B. 100.48

    C. 64.00

    D. 12.56

11) Which of the following is the correct calculation for 7!?

    A. $7 \times 6 \times 5 \times 4 \times 3 \times 2 \times 1$

    B. $1 \times 2 \times 3 \times 4 \times 5 \times 6$

    C. $0 \times 1 \times 2 \times 3 \times 4 \times 5 \times 6 \times 7$

    D. $1 \times 2 \times 3 \times 4 \times 5 \times 6 \times 7 \times 8$

12) The equation of a line is given as: $y = 5x - 3$. Which of the following points does not lie on the line?

   A. (1, 2)
   B. (−2, −13)
   C. (3, 18)
   D. (2, 7)

13) How long is the line segment shown on the number line below?

   A. −9
   B. −8
   C. 8
   D. 9

14) What is the distance between the points (1, 3) and (−2, 7)?

   A. 3
   B. 4
   C. 5
   D. 6

15) $x^2 - 81 = 0$, x could be:

   A. 6
   B. 9
   C. 12
   D. 15

16) A rectangular plot of land is measured to be 160 feet by 200 feet. Its total area is:

   A. 32,000 square feet
   B. 4,404 square feet
   C. 3,200 square feet
   D. 2,040 square feet

17) With what number must 2.103119 be multiplied in order to obtain the number 21,031.19?

   A. 100

   B. 1,000

   C. 10,000

   D. 100,000

18) Which of the following is NOT a factor of 50?

   A. 5

   B. 10

   C. 2

   D. 100

19) The sum of 4 numbers is greater than 320 and less than 360. Which of the following could be the average (arithmetic mean) of the numbers?

   A. 80

   B. 85

   C. 90

   D. 95

20) One fourth the cube of 4 is:

   A. 25

   B. 16

   C. 32

   D. 8

21) What is the sum of the prime numbers in the following list of numbers?

   14, 12, 11, 16, 13, 20, 19, 36, 30

   A. 26

   B. 37

   C. 43

   D. 32

22) Convert 25% to a fraction.

   A. 1/2

   B. 2/3

   C. 1/4

   D. 3/4

23) The supplement angle of a 45° angle is:

   A. 135°

   B. 105°

   C. 90°

   D. 35°

24) 20% of 50 is:

   A. 30

   B. 25

   C. 20

   D. 10

25) Simplify: $5(2x^6)^3$.

   A. $10x^9$

   B. $10x^{18}$

   C. $40x^{18}$

   D. $40x^9$

IF YOU FINISH BEFORE TIME IS CALLED, YOU MAY CHECK YOUR WORK ON THIS SECTION ONLY. DO NOT TURN TO OTHER SECTION IN THE TEST. **STOP**

AFOQT Mathematics Practice Tests

Answers and Explanations

AFOQT Practice Test 1 CAT - ASVAB			
Arithmetic Reasoning		Mathematics Knowledge	
1)	B	1)	C
2)	D	2)	D
3)	D	3)	B
4)	B	4)	A
5)	A	5)	C
6)	C	6)	D
7)	A	7)	B
8)	A	8)	B
9)	C	9)	D
10)	D	10)	A
11)	C	11)	C
12)	A	12)	B
13)	B	13)	C
14)	C	14)	C
15)	B	15)	B
16)	C	16)	B

AFOQT Math Practice Test 2 - Paper and Pencil

Arithmetic Reasoning				Mathematics Knowledge			
1)	D	16)	C	1)	D	16)	C
2)	D	17)	A	2)	D	17)	C
3)	C	18)	C	3)	C	18)	D
4)	C	19)	A	4)	A	19)	B
5)	A	20)	B	5)	A	20)	B
6)	A	21)	C	6)	C	21)	C
7)	B	22)	D	7)	C	22)	C
8)	D	23)	A	8)	B	23)	A
9)	A	24)	D	9)	A	24)	D
10)	A	25)	C	10)	A	25)	C
11)	C	26)	C	11)	A	26)	
12)	A	27)	D	12)	C	27)	
13)	B	28)	B	13)	D	28)	
14)	B	29)	D	14)	C	29)	
15)	B	30)	D	15)	B	30)	

AFOQT Math Practice Tests Explanations

In this section, answers and explanations are provided for two AFOQT Math Tests, Test I CAT-AFOQT and Test 2 Paper and Pencil – ASVAB. Review the answers and explanations to learn more about solving AFOQT Math questions fast.

AFOQT Math Practice Test 1
CAT-AFOQT Arithmetic Reasoning
Answers and Explanations

1) **Choice B is correct**

   $36 \div 3 = 12$ hours for one course

   $12 \times 25 = 300 \Rightarrow \$300$

2) **Choice D is correct**

   Michelle = Karen – 9, Michelle = David – 4, Karen + Michelle + David = 82

   Karen + 9 = Michelle $\quad \Rightarrow$ Karen = Michelle – 9

   Karen + Michelle + David = 82

   Now, replace the ages of Karen and David by Michelle. Then:

   Michelle + 9 + Michelle + Michelle + 4 = 82

   3Michelle + 13 = 82 $\quad \Rightarrow$ 3Michelle = 82 – 13 $\Rightarrow$ 3 Michelle = 69 $\Rightarrow$ Michelle = 23

3) **Choice D is correct**

   $$distance = speed \times time \Rightarrow \text{time} = \frac{distance}{speed} = \frac{600}{50} = 12$$

   (Round trip means that the distance is 600 miles)

   The round trip takes 12 hours. Change hours to minutes, then:

$$12 \times 60 = 720$$

4) Choice B is correct

Since Julie gives 8 pieces of candy to each of her friends, then, then number of pieces of candies must be divisible by 8.

A. 187 ÷ 8 = 23.375
B. 216 ÷ 8 = 27
C. 343 ÷ 8 = 42.875
D. 223 ÷ 8 = 27.875

Only choice b gives a whole number.

5) Choice A is correct

Area of a rectangle = width × length = 30 × 45 = 1,350

6) Choice C is correct

$average = \frac{sum}{total}$, Sum = 2 + 5 + 22 + 28 + 32 + 35 + 35 + 33 = 192

Total number of numbers = 8, $average = \frac{192}{8}$ = 24

7) Choice A is correct

The base rate is $15. The fee for the first 40 visits is: $40 \times 0.20 = 8$

The fee for the visits 41 to 60 is: $20 \times 0.10 = 2$, Total charge: 15 + 8 + 2 = 25

8) Choice A is correct

$$average = \frac{sum}{total} = \frac{32 + 35 + 29}{3} = \frac{96}{3} = 32$$

9) Choice C is correct

The amount they have = $10.25 + $11.25 + $18.45 = 39.95

10) Choice D is correct

Change 9 hours to minutes, then: 9 × 60 = 540 minutes

$\frac{540}{90} = 6$

11) Choice C is correct

15 dozen of magazines are 180 magazines: 15 × 12 = 180

180 − 57 = 123

12) Choice A is correct

$$probability = \frac{desired\ outcomes}{possible\ outcomes} = \frac{4}{4+3+7+10} = \frac{4}{24} = \frac{1}{6}$$

13) Choice B is correct

Find the value of each choice:

    A. 2 × 2 × 5 × 7 = 140

    B. 2 × 2 × 2 × 2 × 5 × 7 = 560

    C. 2 × 7 = 14

    D. 2 × 2 × 2 × 5 × 7 = 280

14) Choice C is correct

1 ton = 2,000 pounds,   5 ton = 10,000 pounds, $\frac{32,000}{10,000} = 3.2$

William needs to make at least 4 trips to deliver all of the food.

15) Choice B is correct

180 − 40 − 50 = 90

16) Choice C is correct

Each worker can walk 3 dogs: 9 ÷ 3 = 3, 5 workers can walk 15 dogs. 5 × 3 = 15

AFOQT Math Practice Test 1
CAT-AFOQT Mathematics Knowledge
Answers and Explanations

1) **Choice C is correct**

   If a = 3 then: b = $\frac{a^2}{3}$ + 3 $\Rightarrow$ b = $\frac{3^2}{3}$ + 3 = 3 + 3 = 6

2) **Choice D is correct**

   $\sqrt[8]{256}$ = 2,   ($2^8 = 2 \times 2 \times 2 \times 2 \times 2 \times 2 \times 2 \times 2 = 256$)

3) **Choice B is correct**

   (r = radius) Area of a circle = πr² = π × (5)² = 3.14 × 25 = 78.5

4) **Choice A is correct**

   $-8a = 64$ $\Rightarrow$ $a = \frac{64}{-8} = -8$

5) **Choice C is correct**

   All angles in a triable add up to 180 degrees.

   90° + 45° = 135°

   x = 180° − 135° = 45°

6) **Choice D is correct**

   Use Pythagorean Theorem: a² + b² = c²

   (4)² + (5)² = c² $\Rightarrow$ 16 + 25 = 41 = C² $\Rightarrow$ C = $\sqrt{41}$ = 6.403

7) **Choice B is correct**

   Use FOIL (first, out, in, last) method.

$(5x + 5)(2x + 6) = 10x^2 + 30x + 10x + 30 = 10x^2 + 40x + 30$

8) Choice B is correct

$5(a-6) = 22 \Rightarrow 5a - 30 = 22 \Rightarrow 5a = 22 + 30 = 52$

$\Rightarrow 5a = 52 \Rightarrow a = \frac{52}{5} = 10.4$

9) Choice D is correct

Use exponent multiplication rule: $x^a \cdot x^b = x^{a+b}$

Then: $3^{24} = 3^8 \times 3^x = 3^{8+x}$, $24 = 8 + x \Rightarrow x = 24 - 8 = 16$

10) Choice A is correct

An obtuse angle is an angle of greater than 90 degrees and less than 180 degrees. Only choice a is an obtuse angle.

11) Choice C is correct

To factor the expression $x^2 + 5 - 6$, we need to find two numbers whose sum is 5 and their product is -6. Those numbers are 6 and -1. Then: $x^2 + 5 - 6 = (x + 6)(x - 1)$

12) Choice B is correct

Slope of a line: $\frac{y_2 - y_1}{x_2 - x_1} = \frac{rise}{run}$, $\frac{y_2 - y_1}{x_2 - x_1} = \frac{3 - 7}{5 - 6} = \frac{-4}{-1} = 4$

13) Choice C is correct

$\sqrt{100} = 10$, $\sqrt{36} = 6$, $10 \times 6 = 60$

14) Choice C is correct

Only choice c is not equal to 5^2

15) Choice B is correct

$\sqrt[3]{2,197} = 13$

16) Choice B is correct

In scientific notation form, numbers are written with one whole number times 10 to the power of a whole number. Number 952,710 has 6 digits. Write the number and after the first digit put the decimal point. Then, multiply the number by 10 to the power of 5 (number of remaining digits). Then:

952,710 = 9.5271×10^5

AFOQT Math Practice Test 2
Paper and Pencil - Arithmetic Reasoning
Answers and Explanations

1) **Choice D is correct**

2 weeks = 14 days, then: 14 × 6 = 84 hours

84 × 60 = 5,040 minutes

2) **Choice D is correct**

$$\text{distance} = \text{speed} \times \text{time} \Rightarrow \text{time} = \frac{\text{distance}}{\text{speed}} = \frac{340 + 340}{50} = 13.6$$

(Round trip means that the distance is 680 miles)

The round trip takes 13.6 hours. Change hours to minutes, then: $13.6 \times 60 = 816$

3) **Choice C is correct**

60 − 42 = 18 male students, $\frac{18}{60} = 0.3$

Change 0.3 to percent ⇒ 0.3 × 100 = 30%

4) **Choice C is correct**

$average = \frac{sum}{total}$, Sum = 7 + 9 + 22 + 28 + 28 + 30 = 124

Total number of numbers = 9, $\frac{124}{6} = 20.67$

5) Choice A is correct

Emma's three best times are 54, 57, and 57. The average of these numbers is:

$average = \frac{sum}{total}$, Sum = 54 + 57 + 57 = 168,   Total number of numbers = 3

$$average = \frac{168}{3} = 56$$

6) Choice A is correct

The area of a 15 feet x 15 feet room is 225 square feet.
15 × 15 = 225

7) Choice B is correct

1.303572 × 1000 = 1303.572

8) Choice D is correct

The factors of 50 are: {1, 2, 5, 10, 25, 50},   15 is not a factor of 50.

9) Choice A is correct

4 percent of 25 is: $25 \times \frac{4}{100} = 1$,   Emma's new rate is 26. 25 + 1 = 26

10) Choice A is correct

Emily = Lucas, Emily = 4 Mia   ⇒ Lucas = 4 Mia, Lucas = Mia + 21

then: Lucas = Mia + 21   ⇒ 4 Mia = Mia + 21,   Remove 1 Mia from both sides of the equation. Then: 3 Mia = 21 ⇒ Mia = 7

11) Choice C is correct

12 days, 12 × 5 = 60 hours, 60 × 60 = 3,600 minutes

12) Choice A is correct

Sum = 22 + 34 + 16 + 20 = 92, $average = \frac{92}{4} = 23$

13) Choice B is correct

Perimeter of a rectangle = 2 × length + 2 × width =

2 × 90 + 2 × 30 = 180 + 60 = 240

14) Choice B is correct

$Speed = \frac{distance}{time}$, $16.2 = \frac{distance}{2.1} \Rightarrow distance = 16.2 \times 2.1 = 34.02$

Rounded to a whole number, the answer is 34.

15) Choice B is correct

Let's review the choices provided and find their sum.

a. 20 × 6 = 120
b. 26 × 6 = 144 ⇒ is greater than 120 and less than 180
c. 30 × 6 = 180
d. 34 × 6 = 204

Only choice b gives a number that is greater than 120 and less than 180.

16) Choice C is correct

$\frac{1 \; hour}{15 \; coffees} = \frac{x}{1500} \Rightarrow 15 \times x = 1 \times 1,500 \Rightarrow 15x = 1,500, \quad x = 100$

It takes 100 hours until she's made 1,500 coffees.

17) Choice A is correct

120 − 12 = 108, $\frac{108}{12} = 9$

18) Choice C is correct

$percent \; of \; change = \frac{change}{original \; number}$, 7.75 − 7.50 = 0.25

$percent \; of \; change = \frac{0.25}{7.50} = 0.0333 \quad \Rightarrow 0.0333 \times 100 = 3.33\%$

19) Choice A is correct

Write a proportion and solve.

$\frac{\frac{1}{2}inches}{4.5} = \frac{1\ mile}{x}$, Use cross multiplication, then: $\frac{1}{2}x = 4.5 \rightarrow x = 9$

20) Choice B is correct

Two candy bars costs 50¢ and a package of peanuts cost 75¢ and a can of cola costs 50¢. The total cost is: 50 + 75 + 50 = 175,   175 is equal to 7 quarters. 7 × 25 = 175

21) Choice C is correct

Every day the hour hand of a watch makes 2 complete rotation. Thus, it makes 16 complete rotations in 8 days. 2 × 8 = 16

22) Choice D is correct

$\sqrt{81} \times \sqrt{25}$ = 9 × 5 = 45

23) Choice A is correct

2y + 4y + 2y = − 24   ⇒ 8y = − 24   ⇒ $y = -\frac{24}{8}$ ⇒ y = − 3

24) Choice D is correct

$2\frac{2}{3} - 1\frac{5}{6} = 2\frac{4}{6} - 1\frac{5}{6} = \frac{16}{6} - \frac{11}{6} = \frac{5}{6}$

25) Choice C is correct

To convert a decimal to percent, multiply it by 100 and then add percent sign (%). 0.023 × 100 = 2.30%

26) Choice C is correct

2 WEEKS = 14 DAYS, 3 hours × 14 Days = 42 hours, 42 hours =2,520 minutes

27) Choice D is correct

180 ÷ 20 = 9

28) Choice B is correct

30% × 50 = $\frac{30}{100}$ × 50 = 15

The coupon has $15 value. Then, the selling price of the sweater is $35. 50 – 15 = 35

Add 5% tax, then: $\frac{5}{100} \times 35 = 1.75$ for tax, then: 35 + 1.75 = $36.75

29) Choice D is correct

1 quart = 0.25 gallon, 34 quarts = 34 × 0.25 = 8.5 gallons, then: $\frac{8.5}{2}$ = 4.25 weeks

30) Choice D is correct

The difference of the file added, and the file deleted is: 652,159 – 599,986 = 52,173

937,036 + 52,173 = 989,209

AFOQT Math Practice Test 2

Paper and Pencil - Mathematics Knowledge

Answers and Explanations

1) Choice D is correct

Use FOIL (First, Out, In, Last) method. $(x + 7)(x + 5) = x^2 + 5x + 7x + 35 = x^2 + 12x + 3$

2) Choice D is correct

In scientific notation form, numbers are written with one whole number times 10 to the power of a whole number. Number 670,000 has 6 digits. Write the number and after the first digit put the decimal point. Then, multiply the number by 10 to the power of 5 (number of remaining digits). Then: $670,000 = 6.7 \times 10^5$

3) Choice C is correct

Perimeter of a triangle = side 1 + side 2 + side 3 = 25 + 25 + 25 = 75

4) Choice A is correct

From the choices provided, 36, 48 and 54 are divisible by 6. From these numbers, 54 is the biggest.

5) Choice A is correct

Oven 1 = 4 oven 2,   If Oven 2 burns 3 then oven 1 burns 12 pizzas. 3 + 12 = 15

6) Choice C is correct

An obtuse angle is an angle of greater than 90° and less than 180°.

7) Choice C is correct

Use exponent multiplication rule: $x^a \cdot x^b = x^{a+b}$

Then: $7^7 \times 7^8 = 7^{15}$

8) Choice B is correct

5231.48245 rounded to the nearest tenth equals 5231.5

(Because 5231.48 is closer to 5,231.5 than 5,231.4)

9) Choice A is correct

$\sqrt[3]{512} = 8$

10) Choice A is correct

Diameter = 16, then: Radius = 8

Area of a circle = πr^2 ⇒ A = 3.14(8)² = 200.96

11) Choice A is correct

7! = 7 × 6 × 5 × 4 × 3 × 2 × 1

12) Choice C is correct

Let's review the choices provided. Put the values of x and y in the equation.

A. (1, 2)   ⇒ $x = 1$ ⇒ $y = 2$ This is true!

B. (−2, −13)   ⇒ $x = -2$ ⇒ $y = -13$ This is true!

C. (3, 18) $\Rightarrow x = 3 \Rightarrow y = 12$ This is not true!

D. (2, 7) $\Rightarrow x = 2 \Rightarrow y = 7$ This is true!

13) Choice D is correct

$1 - (-8) = 1 + 8 = 9$

14) Choice C is correct

Use distance formula:

$d = \sqrt{(x_1 - x_2)^2 + (y_1 - y_2)^2} = \sqrt{(1 - (-2))^2 + (3 - 7)^2}$

$\sqrt{9 + 16} = \sqrt{25} = 5$

15) Choice B is correct

$x^2 - 81 = 0 \Rightarrow x^2 = 81 \Rightarrow x$ could be 9 or –9.

16) Choice C is correct

Area of a rectangle = width × length = 160 × 200 = 3,200

17) Choice C is correct

Number 2.103119 should be multiplied by 10,000 in order to obtain the number 21,031.19

2.103119 × 10,000 = 21,031.19

18) Choice D is correct

factor of 50 = {1, 2, 5, 10, 25, 50}

100 is not a factor of 50.

19) Choice B is correct

Let's review the choices provided.

A. 80 × 4 = 320

B. 85 × 4 = 340

C. 90 × 4 = 360

D. 95 × 4 = 380

From choices provided, only 340 is greater than 320 and less than 360.

20) Choice B is correct

The cube of 4 = 4 × 4 × 4 = 64

$\frac{1}{4}$ × 64 = 16

21) Choice C is correct

From the list of numbers, 11, 13, and 19 are prime numbers. Their sum is:

11 + 13 + 19 = 43

22) Choice C is correct

25% = $\frac{25}{100}$ = $\frac{1}{4}$

23) Choice A is correct

Two Angles are supplementary when they add up to 180 degrees.

135° + 45° = 180°

24) Choice D is correct

$\frac{20}{100}$ × 50 = 10

25) Choice C is correct

$5(2x^6)^3 \Rightarrow 5 \times 2^3 \times x^{18} = 40x^{18}$

"Effortless Math" Publications

Effortless Math authors' team strives to prepare and publish the best quality Mathematics learning resources to make learning Math easier for all. We hope that our publications help you or your student Math in an effective way.

We all in Effortless Math wish you good luck and successful studies!

Effortless Math Authors

www.EffortlessMath.com

... So Much More Online!

✓ FREE Math lessons

✓ More Math learning books!

✓ Mathematics Worksheets

✓ Online Math Tutors

Need a PDF version of this book?

Please visit www.EffortlessMath.com

Made in the USA
Coppell, TX
12 December 2020